Two plays

Salabega and Columbus

Salabega and Columbus

Niladri Bhusan Harichandan

Translated by
Sanjeet Kumar Das

BLACK EAGLE BOOKS
Dublin, USA | Bhubaneswar, India

Black Eagle Books
USA address:
7464 Wisdom Lane
Dublin, OH 43016

India address:
E/312, Trident Galaxy, Kalinga Nagar,
Bhubaneswar-751003, Odisha, India

E-mail: info@blackeaglebooks.org
Website: www.blackeaglebooks.org

First International Edition Published by
Black Eagle Books, 2023

SALABEGA AND COLUMBUS
by **Niladri Bhusan Harichandan**

Translated by **Sanjeet Kumar Das**

Original Copyright © Niladri Bhusan Harichandan
Translation Copyright © Sanjeet Kumar Das

All rights reserved. No part of this publication may be reproduced, stored in a retrieval system, or transmitted, in any form or by any means, electronic, mechanical, photocopying, recording or otherwise without the prior permission of the publisher.

Cover & Interior Design: Ezy's Publication

ISBN- 978-1-64560-485-3 (Paperback)
Library of Congress Control Number: 2023951480

Printed in the United States of America

For
Swopna, my daughter
Sujata, my wife
and
Bapa and Maa

Author's View

Columbus's adventurous and romantic sea voyage and indomitable zeal to explore the 'New Land' or country is concatenated as a fresh chapter to the geographical history of the world. Though Columbus discovered America, it was named after the deceitful tartuffe Amerigo Vespucci. Along with the sufferings of the sea expedition and the apprehensions of life, he has subsequently experienced and overcome the frequent conspiracies plotted against him by his crew members on the ship and the royal court. Columbus marches ahead steadily with his strong mental prowess. He comes across failures time and again. But he has yet to deviate from his path to reach the goal. His only ambition is to discover the 'New Land'. Struggling for a long time in the Atlantic Ocean, he continues his expedition despite the hiccoughs and huddles on his way. To him, life aims to carry on adventurous journeys on sea irresistibly and uncontrollably.

The life of Columbus is flamboyant. More dramatic is his struggling life and exhilarative journey on the sea. The combating spirit, intense desire and apprehensions he encountered help him live life with unbeatable strength and are a humble endeavour made through this play Columbus.

In Odisha's religious world, the non-Hindu poet Salabega has a strange personality. By birth, Salabega is a Muslim, but he is one of the supreme devotees of Lord Jagannath. All his hymns or devotional songs are dedicated to Lord Jagannath. He has not been confined to Islam religion. Though he was a devotee of Jagannath, he couldn't be a Hindu throughout his life. He is prohibited from entering Jagannath Temple, Puri. Being trapped on the horns of the dilemma, he suffers a lot and plans for a new religion. Later, he named it the 'Religion of Humanity' and the natural outcome of that time. The play declares that, having been released from narrow parochialism and blind beliefs of caste and religion, Salabega has come forward irresistibly to propagate and establish his religion worldwide. To him, this 'Religion of Humanity' is true and eternal. He has consistently followed the path of righteousness. Wandering between two main religions, the mental strife or agonies he has undergone are the stuff for me in creating characters like Salabega. With a poetic sensibility and soul, this play has been scripted and published for the larger audience of the world.

Prof. Niladri Bhusan Harichandan

Translator's View

Man's descent on earth is closely related to society and Nature. By God's grace, a man can lead a healthy life in both personal and social spheres. Without struggle, the life of the man becomes impossible. The man must be sound in his mind and body to battle. Mental strength and moral courage are the guiding forces of an individual to move ahead. These will help the individual fight against the evil practices stigmatized in society for so long and the bad habits rooted thoroughly in succession. Every individual's arrival to this society at any part of the world and at any time ascertains a purpose. Everything is pre-decided and run as per the ordeals of God, the Almighty, that can't be forfeited at first glance so easily. When the man completes his work on this mundane firmament, he has to leave for the other world. So, the individual has to be brave enough to raise his voice against social oddities or natural calamities while traversing the route. The hostile forces trending against the individual sometimes become heavy and challenging, while these will accelerate him positively at other times.

Here, I have attempted to club two crucial characters, Salabega and Columbus, well-figured in pages of history by placing them side by side, as a translator to render English translations of the Odia plays Satya Samshaya Salabega as Salabega and Columbus as Columbus of Prof. Nilandri Bhusan Harichandan. The themes of both books appealed to me. So, I started translating them. The language used in both the Odia texts will engage the readers fascinated from the first to the last.

In the book's first part, the character Salabega is by birth a Muslim but a supreme devotee of Lord Jagannath. He hails from a very affluent family. He leads the life of a pauper and, later on, the life of an ascetic. He is known worldwide as a saint-poet of Odia Literature of the first decade of 17th century Odisha. His life gets initially forked between two religions as his father, Lalbega, is a Muslim and his mother, Tulasi, is a Hindu woman. He was not allowed to enter the temple of Lord Jagannath. But, when he is fully aware of the diseased societies and how groundless stereotypes and stigmas control them, he revolts against them and gets alienated with time. He observes that each religion centres on some superstitions and parochial ideals. He says confidently before the parents and deserting home as a wayfarer moves across the length and breadth of India to establish a new religion as the 'Religion of Humanity'. Salabega hammers upon the loopholes and pitfalls of Hindu and Muslim faiths and convinces his parents of these problems. Voicing against the age-old traditional belief system, he undertakes arduous tasks. His strong willpower helps him succeed in the battle against society. The power to succumb to tremendous social pressure is not with every individual. The ones who are blessed with the combating zeal are the iconoclasts to make history for the rest to follow. They are revered as heroic spirits throughout the world. Salabega moves on the path of righteousness to lead a spiritual journey.

In the book's second part, I dealt with the protagonist

Columbus deftly. This historical character is sandwiched between social pressures and natural calamities. He discovered America, but it was named after Amerigo Vespucci. To actualize his explorative zeal, Columbus, in the 15th-century Europe, approached the Kings and the Queens of Portugal, Italy and England but failed everywhere. Finally, the Emperor Ferdinand and Empress Isabella of Spain believed in his inner strength and respected him for sponsoring all sorts of facilities. Others in the Royal Court oppose him strongly before he sets off the odyssey for the 'New Land'. Similar kind of pressure Columbus bears while sailing the ships in the deep ocean. Nature has been insensitive to his scientific desire to discover something extraordinary.

All of them fought bravely against the Natural Calamities. His crew members on the ships plot brutal conspiracies against him. He was a familiar navigator. He tolerated them all and became a morale booster. Despite the warnings and threats of his fellow beings on the vessels, he didn't return to the Native Land. The ordinary people are generally seen to be governed by some ill omens and superstitions while on the sea expedition. Their excitement is eye-catching when they encounter something new towards their sea voyage's end. He closely marks them and calmly proceeds on his way for the more significant interest of the country. His nationalistic zeal earnestly needs a salute.

At last, the Spaniards reached their destination and hoisted the flag of Spain with great ecstasy and exaltation. The moral lesson garnered here is that failure is the pillar of success. We have to struggle until we reach our goal. God tests an individual through pressure exerted either by the populace or by Nature. One who bears it with a big heart wins the race and crowns himself with the success of victory. Everywhere, he becomes the celebrated hero forever. The anthropocentric view of life that 'science outwits Nature' is marked in Columbus.

I have tried my best to keep the language as lucid as possible. While following the rules of equivalence and the rules of fidelity between the Odia language and the English language, I came across some natural shifts. The culture-specific terms of the source language texts are maintained as they are. Some deictic expressions of the Odia language are marked in the target language while translating.

I deeply revere Professor Niladri Bhusan Harichandan for believing me to translate his texts scrupulously. A renowned professor of Odia Literature, he retired from Vishwa-Bharati University. I convey my gratitude to Dr. Alok Kumar Baral, Assistant Professor, Department of Odia Language and Literature, Central University of Odisha, for helping me select these two texts for the stuff of my work.

I convey my heartfelt gratitude to Sri Satya Pattanaik, the director of Black Eagle Books, USA and Sri Ashok Parida of the publishing house for their kind consent to publish the texts in time.

Sanjeet Kumar Das

Critic's View

The translator Sanjeet Kumar Das has beautifully rendered two famous Odia plays, Satya Samsaya Salabega, published in 1981 (as Salabega), and Columbus, published in 1990 (as Columbus) of the playwright Professor Niladri Bhusan Harichandan into English. Both these plays are successful and centre around different protagonists in different set-ups and historical backgrounds. Going beyond the historical boundaries of the last part of the sixteenth century, Salabega transforms himself as an able representative in Contemporary life. Salabega's devotional surrender is interspersed with suspicion and spiritualism before the Almighty and humbly reproduced in this dramatic genre. Breaking the religious sphere and familial conflicts, Salabega wanders freely on this earth for the spread of world-humanity, immersed in the free path of self-sacrifice. Salabega's spiritual journey is forever the self-introspection of Truth and Supernaturalism. "I have loved both the God of the Hindus and the God of the Muslims with my heart and soul. One's formless idol attracts me, while another's void form has appealed to me, too. But I am neither a Hindu nor a Muslim." Salabega's father is a Muslim, whereas his mother is a Hindu woman. He is far above the narrow parochialism of religion and a balanced individual in irrelevant lifestyles. For her mother, he has pure sanctified feelings, and following his father's course of life, Salabega has evolved as reclusive, however diseased and intensely doubtful, and at last stands conspicuously bright and glitter like gold. The apprehensions of life and religion, the suspicions towards Hindu and Muslim faiths, not being inebriated and amassed in wealth and prosperity, Salabega gets inclined towards Lord Jagannath as a supreme devotee. Salabega has metamorphosed himself from the historical backdrop for the discovery of an eternal Truth to which he is entirely dedicated- a historical myth-character.

Accordingly, the glorious efforts of Christopher Columbus as the Italian-born 'Sea Emperor' in the play are well-attempted without obscuring the drama of sea voyages. Defeating the dangerous sea and Nature, staying for a long time on an abandoned island and lonely sea beach, and struggling with moral courage, the sea traveller spends his last time in woes and agonies. In 1502, Columbus set out with his brother and son in four ships on his far-flung voyage. His dream of discovering gold in India has yet to come to fruition. Columbus, who could conquer Nature, was defeated by the Mexicans and was sick of food and Natural disasters. Columbus came back to Spain. In this historical story of Columbus's infinite patience and impossible journey, the dramatist has searched for a rare feeling of drama and theatre. Homeless Columbus's hunger and struggle for life on the earth and the sea have been foregrounded as the central thought of the drama. Defeat is impossible for the victor Columbus. Columbus asks his brother Bartholomew before his death to narrate the heroic story of his triumphant all-round expedition, and he will take that soft complacency and resignation with him into the other world.

The Playwright Niladri Bhushan Harichandan later wrote several biographical plays. From that point of view, one can recall the list of dramas centred on Kuntala Kumari-Nagendrabala-Ashwanikumar. In these dramas, Shakespearean long dialogues with a free flow of thought and parallel creation of tragedy can be available in Niladri Bhushan's style. Not just conceptually but discussed based on dialogues and diction, both Salabega and Columbus are different plays. Correspondingly, the translator Mr Das's selection, coordination, and command over prosaic form are in tune with the original plays.

I greet my 'heartfelt congratulations' to the author and the translator on this occasion. Translation always takes the work into a larger perspective and dramatically increases its readability.

Dr. Alok Baral
Central University of Odisha

DRAMATIS PERSONAE

Play Salabega

Salabega
Lalbega
Tulasi
Vaishnab
Fakir

SALABEGA

[From the background is heard a song. That song is a hymn sung by a Vaishnab -"*Ahe Nila Shaila Prabala Matta Baarana...*" Salabega comes running before the last humming ends. By that time, the Vaishnab comes out from the opposite direction.]

Salabega : Who...? Who is singing this song? Stop it!

Vaishnab : It's not an ordinary song. It's a prayer (a devotional song) and an earnest request of a devotee to God!

Salabega : That's why I am telling you to stop!

Vaishnab : You are telling an extraordinary story. People become mad to hear this hymn. Being overwhelmed by devotion, they drop their tears.

Salabega : Some others can shed tears, but I can't. I don't like this type of surrender before God. Man's individuality is not reflected here. Will he only surrender at the lotus feet of God as a devotee? Can he not gather his power to fight against a trivial ordeal? Will he surrender before God for help, saying "Save me...save me"? As if a motherless child had been searching for a shelter for ages!

Vaishnab : Man is more helpless than a motherless child! Perhaps you don't realize this. That terrible helplessness!

Salabega : If man believes in his power and is determined to overcome the perils and obstacles in life, then...

Vaishnab : No, you have misconceived. Only the poor and distressed invoke God when

		there is misery and a wrong time of life. Is this your idea? But why do you forget, having been prosperous in all life directions, a man often feels helpless and lonely as if he were an animal carrying loads alone in a dreary desert?
Salabega	:	Still, there is happiness in that walking; there is also excitement because then he is not seeking anybody's help and begging before others for compassion. He is not bearing others' hate and disapproval.
Vaishnab	:	If you understand the essence of this hymn,...
Salabega	:	I have understood it very well. If anybody falls in danger and suffers, sincerely cries for help out of distress, God rescues that fellow! As if God wanted, there would be no danger in the world.
Vaishnab	:	It's not a matter of joke. You may need to be made aware of this writing. It is of the supreme Muslim devotee Salabega of Lord Jagannatha. Singing this prayer, he recovered completely from the incurable disease. He was the son of the most powerful *Subedar* (Ruler) of Cuttack province, the Great Lalbega! What was the dearth? But for this disease, he was thrown away mercilessly from his Royal palace.
Salabega	:	Salabega is timid...a coward! Why did he not revolt while he was driven away? Why did he come crying to take shelter under a tree? What was the need to show

devotion to his father in a heartless, inconsiderate society? The father, who was always intoxicated in wine and women, fulfilling his evil intentions, and hoarding his wealth, name and fame, inconsiderably being engaged in murdering the people...plundering, and unleashing pain to the heart, didn't think of Salabega's plight at least once. (Silence)...rightly done...It's the suitable punishment for Salabega! The right decision of inconsideration!!

Vaishnab : That's of Lord Jagannath's *Leelakhela* (tactful amusement)! Had he not been punished so, how would he be worshipped today in the world? Otherwise, doing theft and robbery, he would have increased the sinful activities...

Salabega : Is Salabega worshipped? Astonishment! Who is more sinful than him? Had he not undergone this extreme condition of life, he would not have gained this spiritual consciousness!

Vaishnab : He is not a sinner now. He is now dazzling beautifully like pure gold after being burnt in the fire of realization. God has pardoned him. Otherwise, how could the soul-pleasing words (Full of nectar) have sprung from his heart and soul?

Salabega : Soul-pleasing, full of nectar! Salabega's hymn is then full of nectar! Is it true that the song propagates the ripples

		of spiritualism in the hearts of men and women? No, is this only a bigotry/fanaticism? In one delusion,...
Tulasi	:	(Entering) What's this Salabega? Don't you feel this? How are you telling bigotry to spiritualism? Who can understand spiritualism better than you?
Vaishnab	:	(Being astonished) Who? Are you Salabega? Are you that supreme devotee of Lord Jagannath? I am blessed and happy to see you!
Salabega	:	Who is Salabega? Am I? No, I am a heretic! I am a mean *jabana* (a Muslim).
Tulasi	:	What are you saying, my son? If you say so, I will be hurt. You need help understanding this.
Salabega	:	*Maa* (Mother), I am speaking the Truth! Revolving in the darkness of ignorance today, I have discovered the Truth.
Vaishnab	:	That you have discovered the Truth is rehearsing the whole world. Still, why are you demeaning yourself? Why is this discontentment in a supreme devotee like you?
Salabega	:	Discontentment! My discontentment! Yes, I am speaking of my discontent. But how can you understand my displeasure? Where is contentment in the world?
Vaishnab	:	It's certainly here. To think of God is the supreme cause of extreme bliss of human life.
Tulasi	:	I have sheltered at the feet of God with that thought, my son! Looking at you,

	I have forgotten all my enjoyment and possessions. Today, you are in this condition. (Her eyes are full of tears.) Who is more unfortunate and helpless than me in the world? I became a widow before I understood what life is. While burdened with the pressure of society, your father forcefully took from the bathed place (of a river) a helpless widow, Brahmini. I accepted all my sufferings and agonies. I gave birth to you. I thought, all my nightmares are gone. But,...
Vaishnab :	What's that 'but'? You are most respected as the mother of the holy soul Salabega! Because of you, there has been an excellent transformation of Salabega.
Salabega :	I obey and realize that I have been changed. But what was the need for this change? Today, this change has made me most unhappy. I am asking today, "Who am I? What's my existence? With whom have I the blood relationship? Is it with God? Is it with my father or my mother? I don't have any link with anybody. I am loitering like a planet derailed from the orbit!" (Silent) Can you speak Vaishnab Gosain, whether I am Hindu or Muslim? Whose blood flows in my body?
Tulasi :	Oh! Again, that old question! No, there should not be any doubt or conflict in your mind regarding this.
Salabega :	There is no end to the conflict, *Maa*! Conflicts can continue till the last moment

		of life. It often comes to my mind that my life is very frustrated and ridiculed. Then, what's my goal? Where am I from? Where am I moving continuously…? Why?
Tulasi	:	Yes, I can answer you. You can remember your past! The blood-thirsty Lalbega was using you for his interest and selfishness. He cruelly drove you away from his home when you fell and hurt in the horse-riding, and there was no hope of your recovery. For this only, he lost all his hopes and aspirations from you. Plundering the wealth and money from others, you would not have helped him prosper in life-enjoyment.
Salabega	:	Leave that all, *Maa*! I am destined to suffer. Unnecessarily, why are you blaming my father?
Tulasi	:	What can I do more to a sanguinary barbarous person except blame, Salabega? Not a single letter of my utterance is false. Have you yet to realize this? Today, I also remember when I extinguished the fire of anguish in my heart for my whole life. When I was in youth, he was plunging at me like an insect blinded. As my beauty diminishes gradually, he has thrown me into the road like a withered flower. Has he ever inquired how I am living? Today, that inhuman is mad to run after wine and women. However, his wife and son are sheltering under a tree…
Vaishnab	:	All these are of *Chakadola*, Lord

		Jagannath's wishes, *Maa*. God is he! At his wishes are all his creation and their agonies and happiness!
Tulasi	:	No! I can't tolerate all this! I accept death a hundred times better than spending life like this. When all my past is remembered, my heart gets bruised and shattered in pain! My heart gets bruised...! (Crying, she enters inside.)
Salabega	:	Don't weaken me, Maa! The anguish of the heart is truly unbearable. Am I a devotee of Lord Jagannatha, the God of the poor and distressed? If he is *Bhabagrahi* (One who understands everybody's emotions), who understands the minds of devotees, why has he not pulled me to him? Why... why am I staying as a mean *Jabana* for my whole life? Would I not be stepped up beyond the *jabantwa* (foreignness)?
Vaishnab	:	You have been elevated to the peak by your spiritual power? Everybody confesses freely and openly today. You are the supreme devotee of Lord Jagannath, Salabega!!
Salabega	:	Are the people who accept not deceiving themselves? Are they telling this from their hearts or expressing it from their throats?
Vaishnab	:	Why are you with this suspicion?
Salabega	:	Had I been thought of as the supreme devotee, I might not have been untouchable as the mean *jabana* (foreigner) today. I could have entered

the Jagannath Temple! They have the full right to enter Jagannath Temple as they are the Hindus. If I go on pouring all my offerings, devotions and love of my heart, I don't have that right. Why? I meditate continuously, keeping fasting and penance with austerity, but I can't achieve that right. Then, please speak. Am I wrong in my words?

Vaishnab : No, though you cannot enter the temple, you are deprived of the unending compassion of Lord Jagannath.

Salabega : Why are you making me waver here and there, Vaishnab? Jagannatha is the *Patitapabana* (the saviour of the fallen and sinful). He has infinite compassion for the fallen and sinful. Again, dwelling in the blue caves, he preaches the importance of equality and fraternity! Still then,...

Vaishnab : Jagannath is not responsible for this. He wants everybody to come, but behind all this are some superstitions of our Hindu religion. Man creates the obstacles, not God!

Salabega : Can you remove this superstition? It's impossible. It has not been possible for ages. How can it be possible today? The Badapandas of the Hindu religion, the established people of the society, being well-placed in higher posts, will be directing the community. They are going to control the faith the way they want. For their self-interest, they will

		forget spiritualism and humanism! Who is distancing the devotee from God? Who is making the devotee the fallen?
Vaishnab	:	But they are,...
Salabega	:	It's not 'but'. For this, I have a strong 'dislike' for the Muslim religion. I am neither a Hindu nor a Muslim. [A fakir (a Muslim mendicant) enters.]
Fakir	:	What's this? You can't be a Hindu. You are a Muslim. In your body flows the blood of a Muslim. Can you deny that?
Salabega	:	I am not in a state of accepting and rejecting something.
Fakir	:	Disturbed and distracted till this day, you are roaming here and there aimlessly! You have not explored the Truth. Today, I have come to make you aware of that Truth. Please come with me as a true Muslim. You will undoubtedly gain the supreme Truth and Allah's continuous stream of compassion!
Salabega	:	But for me, all the doors of His compassion are closed. I am already known worldwide as the supreme devotee of the Hindu God, Lord Jagannatha. How can I be considered again as the devotee of Allah?
Fakir	:	Why not? Kalapahada was also a stern, devout Muslim. He was strongly inclined towards the Muslim religion, having been indifferent to the Hindu religion. As a result, he promised to destroy Hindu temples and Hindu Gods and Goddesses.

Vaishnab	:	Your accidental presence is here illogical. You are trying to distract the mind of the devout devotee Salabega unnecessarily.
Fakir	:	I am not distracting. All my words are clear, like sunlight. A Muslim child can't be a *Kafer* (Non-Muslim) at any point. It's impossible to disobey and deny the Order of Allah.
Salabega	:	I may be a Muslim by birth, but I don't have any faith in it. Is one forced to obey a religion by his birth? I am not ready to uphold the traditional way of thinking that the son of a Hindu will be a Hindu, and the son of a Muslim will be a Muslim. I have enough respect for you, and I have enough love for you. Still, I have never accepted the Muslim religion consciously. Why a child's horoscope is is linked with a religion's belief systems? Can an innocent newborn baby decide the superiority and prosperity of a religion? How can one naturally be consecrated in one faith without knowing anything?
Vaishnab	:	Fakir, you see how Salabega's arguments are irrefutable. If anybody has developed any inclination for the Hindu religion, he can't join any other religion. The Hindu religion is the *Sanatan* religion.
Salabega	:	Your arguments are distracting me. Vaishnab, you can speak, "Have I ever accepted the Hindu religion?"
Fakir	:	You are right, Salabega. Over you, I have

		full right. You are the right heir of the great Muslim religion.
Salabega	:	Oh...! Please don't irritate me by talking about religion time and again. I have loved both the souls of the Hindu God and the Muslim God. I have been attracted towards the formless mysterious statue on one side, and on the other side, I have been pleased with the concept and nature of *'shunya'* (Void). At different points, I have been influenced by some features of some religions. I have loved the greatness of both religions. Hence, it's clear from this that I am neither a Hindu nor a Muslim. To me, all religions are equal.
Fakir	:	What do you say? Will the hopes and convictions we have for you be ruined?
Salabega	:	I am neither of anybody's hope nor of anybody's conviction. Why are you pulling me to both sides? Today, I don't hesitate since I have drunk the poison of religion like *Neelakantha* (Lord Shiva). I have already spent one half of my life as a true Muslim and the other half as a true Hindu. But today, I am free from all sorts of cultural purifications! I have indeed been completely drowned in all religions, but I can't be touched and influenced by the holy water of any religion.
Vaishnab	:	No...no, it's impossible. We can't believe you have no attachment to the Hindu religion now. Wherever you may be, not a single Hindu can forget you. The

		hymn '*Ahe Neela Shaila*' has created an unprecedented spiritual vibration in people's hearts. On this pretext, you are the most loved one in every Hindu's heart.
Salabega	:	Oh…! Don't try to ruin and devastate my strong oath that I have already taken, Vaishnab. You go and let me leave alone for a while. Let me think a lot. I have to petrify my heart like a useless stone…I have to make myself strong.
Vaishnab	:	I am leaving but can never forget this accidental companionship with you. If I ever meet you in future, I will be delighted. [Exit]
Salabega	:	*Dharma…Dharma…Dharma!!* A dark, smoky *dharma* (religious) sphere has eclipsed the whole world.
Fakir	:	Please make me clear what your religion is. I came to you to invite to the discourse of the Muslim religion. Having been here, I see a perversion or a transformation of your mind.
Salabega	:	No, I am not perverted. All my unsteady thoughts are moving towards a steady point. I can feel this. This state of happiness has come to my mind after a massive typhoon. Yes, your need is also fulfilled. You may go now.
Fakir	:	But I came here with a message from your father. His mind has been softened with compassion for you. He wants to

		take you back. At a distance, he is eagerly waiting for you.
Salabega	:	Why eagerness? He could have come here.
Fakir	:	No, he did not like sending any of his councilors…
Salabega	:	Oh…! I understood that there would be harm to the aristocracy of Subedar Lalbega. I am grateful to him as he has remembered me.
Fakir	:	Leave that. Please tell me whether you are ready to go with me and to meet your father.
Salabega	:	Impossible! You go now. I don't need that paternal affection. I have entirely forgotten that he might have loved me at some point. Why will I expect that which I have been deprived of for a long time? You will tell my father that Salabega has enough power to live in society. That power is not demoniacal but spiritual. Salabega is not helpless and handicapped. He has earlier received enough heartfelt paternal love.
Fakir	:	Well, all right. (Attempt to leave)
Salabega	:	Listen to me! You will also tell him that he won't meet me again in his lifetime. Now, I have transcended the boundary of earthly love and attachment. I am far above all kinds of attachments. Now you can go.
Fakir	:	Alright, let me go. [Exit]

Salabega	:	(He is walking disturbed for a while. There is an internal conflict in his mind.) Oh…! What shall I do now? I can't finalize what to do. Why can't I come to a final decision? Is it tough to cut off this relationship? To what religion can I cut off? Only religion…religion… religion! One belief is fighting with other religions! But, nowhere is the question of spiritualism.
Tulasi	:	(Entering) My child, why are you always shouting religion, religion like a lunatic? Sometimes, you are entirely absorbed in devotion to God; sometimes, like an atheist, you are saying uselessly.
Salabega	:	I am on the horns of dilemma, *Maa*! I can't decide what to do. Every moment, many distracted thoughts make me unsteady and disturbed. On one side, there is an uninvited call of an unknown divine power; on the other, there is an infinite stream of soft maternal love. Which one of these two can I leave? An inexpressible delusion fastens me every moment like a *nagaphasha*. (A kind of noose used in the battle to capture an enemy.) There is no way to get out of it. *Maa*, what can I do? Tell me the way out of it, *Maa*. Salabega is shouting like a newborn baby of those days for your assurance. Today, he is extending his hands to the void for help at a critical moment in life.

		[He cries.]
Tulasi	:	(Shouting) Salabega! What are you saying? Of what power are you attracted? As a result, your mother's love and affection have become trivial and insignificant.
Salabega	:	No, *Maa*, don't hike my pressure of sorrows by saying so. Salabega is not ungrateful to you, *Maa*. If he leaves home searching for the Truth, his mother's compassionate figure will be floated in his heart every moment.
Tulasi	:	What are you saying? Will you leave your ever-unhappy mother alone? What mistake have I made to you? Speak... speak; otherwise, I will die thrashing my head at your feet. [She cried.]
Salabega	:	Don't worry like this, *Maa*! Why will you make any mistake? All mistakes are mine. Can a good and promising mother like you think of any evil for her son? However, you have brought me back from a deathbed. Can I ever deny that? No, I can't stay leaving you.
Tulasi	:	My son! You won't be so obstinate ever. Can't you know that this hurts me? You are not getting a little peace and consolation from this pauper, so you are...(Silent) Where is the King's palace, and where is the shed to shelter under a tree? Knowingly, you have kicked everything with your feet!
Salabega	:	I didn't need anything, *Maa*. I was revolving around a blind vortex up to this

day. I didn't get any support anywhere. I have reached ashore because of my fate. Is it not a hundred times better to rest under a tree to see the open sky and enjoy the cool breeze than inauspicious luxurious living, *Maa*?

Tulasi : All these are good to an unfortunate pauper like me. I love them all sincerely. But for you, my mind gets stirred and moved. If the elephant stays in the forest, it is for the King's only. How can I not look for your happiness when I have given birth to you? There you were, staying happily. There was food, dress, care and service! (Silent) Where are those days when you were clad in prince attire, accommodated at the palace and given respect and prestige? Today, your identity is the son of an unprotected, helpless female beggar.

Salabega : Why are you worried unnecessarily, *Maa*? Have I ever told you that I would like all those. The present situation appeals to me a lot. My birth was not for sleeping in *a hamsuli* (made of the soft feathers of a swan) bed. My birth is to stay under a tree to explore the Truth that the open sky and storm are giving away.

Tulasi : I bless you, my son! You will undoubtedly come across that Truth...Due to the unending compassion of Lord Jagannath, you have been fully recovered. You will

	get back your previous energy/ power very shortly.
Salabega :	But I pray to Lord Jagannatha to rejuvenate me with devotion instead of power. This power is the root cause of all forms of cruelties and callousness we see worldwide. I can only reach the over-soul (the supreme power) through my devotion. At some lonely moments, alone in a state of helplessness, I can attain that which one can deeply realize and under whose spell both mind and soul get fulfilled with a divine sublime peace and tranquility.
Tulasi :	Lord Jagannath has never unfulfilled anybody's wishes. He has also heard the call of this unfortunate mother. He is *Bhabagrahi* (One understands sense and appreciates sentiments) and *Patitapabana* (One helps the fallen and the sinful). When you sheltered, meditating at His feet, keeping all your hopes and convictions aside, Lord Jagannath came to you, leaving *Bada Deula* (the Great Temple). Having touched your body, he recovered you.
Salabega :	Absolutely, *Maa*! It was a great surprise! I had given up all my hopes to recover from this disease. I have never thought of it in dreams. Is Lord Jagannath the Truth? Did he listen to me? I can't believe that. The degree of my suspicion increases day by day.

Tulasi	:	How you can't believe it! There is a great chasm between your past and present life. Are you unable to realize that? One day, you had lost your humanity and sensibility and petrified into an atheist and a sinner. Having kicked Mother Earth, you were dripping blood from her heart. Today, looking at this Earth-Mother, your poetic sense springs up spontaneously. In your recitation of devotional songs, the trees and creepers are pleased. They are listening to your heartfelt devotion, the elixir of life, dedicated to the divine soul in silence very anxiously!
Salabega	:	A strange transformation in the true sense! My whole body shivers when I recollect the earlier days of my life. I was behaving like a wild creature in those days! I was trying to ruin the ever-human-creation, attached to the false pride! Who is Hindu? Again, who is Muslim? In every individual flows the Supreme Soul's holy blood (*Parama Pita*). But why is there so much hatred and enmity? Is it the goal of human birth?
Tulasi	:	At that time, I condemned myself a hundred times and thought that giving birth to a cursed child was a distress. But today, I feel proud of you. Lord Jagannath has heard me.
Salabega	:	But I think, had I not been hurt, bruised, and bedridden that day, would the darkness inculcated in my mind have

		been removed? Would I have received the search of that brightened ever-lit moon? (Silent) When the lamp of my life dimmed gradually at my deathbed, all the people lost their hopes for me. I could not hear the sound of anybody's footsteps near my bed. My father was engrossed in wine and women, when I was utterly helpless and shattered. The jingling of the anklet worn by Zaib-un-Nisa, my father's concubine, was heard at a distance better than the distressed cry of my dying stage, then as if my heart were cut into pieces by the saw. My mind revolted. An unending storm stirred in my heart. Can you imagine how more painful that can be than the death?
Tulasi	:	Ah...! Don't tell me all this. Hearing this, I will be mad. I feel giddy now.
Salabega	:	No, that anguish may be more painful; however, it was an unseen blessing of the Almighty for me. Had it not been the cause, how could I see the difference between virtue and vice, truth and falsehood, justice and injustice? In time, I became firm in my mind and body. I forgot all the days of my bitter experience. Then, I realized that I was floating toward a different world. That's why I didn't pay any attention to the cruelties of my father. Instead, I had made myself as strong as thunder.
Tulasi	:	Don't speak unnecessarily, my son! Past

		is passed. Will you gain anything, if you recollect your past? You are already on the path of righteousness. That's my beauty and prosperity. Take a rest peacefully.
Salabega	:	How will I take a rest, *Maa*? I have received a call for a long pilgrimage (a march on foot). How can I avoid that call? However, I don't know where the endpoint of this long march on foot is.
Tulasi	:	What are you saying? Is it a long journey on foot? Can your body bear? Why have you stored all this in your mind as soon as you get up from the bed?
Salabega	:	For how many days will you fasten me as a treasure or storehouse of this region? Your love and service have brought me back from the clutch of death today. (Silent) I had forgotten this colourless earth by the charismatic touch of the unconditional love of my mother, trapped in deep distress. I thought I was an innocent child of the past, sleeping in a bed with eyes towards the mother and playing with hands and legs stretched. What a heavenly bliss! Can I get back my lost childhood days of innocence again?
Tulasi	:	The childhood life can't return, my son! But, earlier experiences can come back. The child's tender feelings, simplicity and innocence can return if one wants…
Salabega	:	Is it possible?
Tulasi	:	Why not? Your absolute devotion to Lord Jagannatha has touched me and surprised

me frequently. Because of the influence of this pure devotion, has your heart not become the heart of a child? You can't see this, but the new buds spread worldwide. Your devotional songs are lively, ever-life-giving force, nectar-like sweet, and the source of all kinds of emotions. Won't Jagannath descend from the "Ratnavedi" (the Raised Platform on which the images of Jagannath, Balabhadra and Subhadra and the emblem of Sudarshan are installed.), having heard your hymns?

Salabega : But...but even once, I cannot see Him. Can He not run to me in that form of *Balagopal*? Playing with Him, I could have forgotten all the world's pains, sufferings, distresses and agonies. I can start dancing like an innocent child enjoying the heavenly bliss.

Tulasi : If you call Him with the mind of a child, my son, you can undoubtedly see Him in the form of a child. He is a mystery. All forms are possible for Him. The way you show your devotion to Him, he will be seen or visible to you in that form.

Salabega : Truly, mysterious is the idol of Lord Jagannath. It does not have hands and legs, and eyes and nose. He has only two big, rounded eyes. It's supernatural. Does the idol symbolize any form or formless? God's statue is not imagined here in human form. Everything is void, devoid of structure. Sometimes, one particular

		form of Him is conceived in the eyes, and sometimes not. That form is visible for a second and then gets lost.
Tulasi	:	That idol is immutable and inevitable. Try to surrender your mind and body at His feet. One day, you will see him standing before you lively in one form.
Salabega	:	I am waiting for that auspicious day, *Maa*. Because of your virtuous soul, my eyes are open and lit with proper knowledge.
Tulasi	:	Your eyes are the colour of the early morning sun. The world is beautifully brightened and lively in that colour. [Look at this (pointing with finger), in the faces of both mother and son is the emotion of novel great fulfilment.]
Salabega	:	But Maa...I understand all I know. I feel and realize everything in my body. But why does a dark murky night of suspicion cover my heart the next moment, *Maa*?
Tulasi	:	What are you saying again, Salabega? How are you changed every moment? Just before a few seconds, you were absorbed in divine thoughts. But what's this now? I have marked you for the last few days; you are unsteady and perplexed by your heart. What you think at one moment is completely changed the next moment. Where do these evil thoughts come to your mind? There is no cause, but? Tell me...tell me frankly, if you have a little love and affection for your mother, express it without any hesitation.

Salabega	:	How can I make you understand all this, *Maa*? I know very well that your simple heart is hurt severely by the accidental change of my mind. But, I am helpless, *Maa*.
Tulasi	:	You are trying to hide something from me, Salabega! I don't have any relatives in the society...I don't have anything- I am staying here looking at your moon-like face. What's the need of my life now? It is better to leave the world than to live with the agonies of a cow without her calf.
Salabega	:	(Shouting) *Maa*! (He caught hold of her hands with tearful eyes.) Salabega is not deceitful and treacherous to his mother. Can he forget his mother's unconditional love and affection for her entire life? (Silent) In an inauspicious moment, I touched this dusky earth as a newborn for the first time. As a traveler or wanderer who has lost his path, I was moving around, aimlessly searching for the way. But where's the course? From a distance what is seen to my eyes as a path is being lost amidst the wild thorny bushes, while I come closer to it. Again, I am moving. There is no end to this search. (Eagerly) *Maa*! You are the person to show me that path. For that only, I will be indebted to you for my entire life, *Maa*! This is not only the gratefulness of a son for his birth to his mother but an uncommon quenchless thirst for spiritual life!

Tulasi	:	I know that as soon as you recover from your illness, a strong storm has erupted in your mind. That storm is for the eternal light. You have already got that light. Today, you are respected worldwide as one of the supreme devotees of Lord Jagannath. Then, what's the need of being a saint? Why are you so anxious?
Salabega	:	I was blind. It was perfect, *Maa*! Why did you open my eyes and show me the stream of infinite light? Who is happier than a blind man in this world, *Maa*? To accept all the evil and inauspicious events of the world in imaginary eyes as the source of compassion, like the blind man, is very heart-touching and consoling. But today, the eyes of Salabega are open. He has become the unhappiest person in the world. Are you not responsible for this?
Tulasi	:	What are you saying, Salabega? Because of me, how can you be unhappy if you have explored and attained the Truth? Instead, you are the happiest person in the world.
Salabega	:	That truth you have helped me attain, and you feel proud of it, is not the Truth, *Maa*. Above this Truth, there is also another Greater Truth of which you are unaware. This is the first time I have experienced this.
Tulasi	:	Then, I am fortunate. If you have explored that ultimate Truth, as your mother, I will be the proudest person in the world.

	I don't have any divine knowledge. I can't go beyond this finite boundary. To surrender entirely at the feet of Lord Jagannath, I have accepted as the Real Truth and Religion of my life. Except that, I don't know anything more.
Salabega :	I had also surrendered myself completely before Allah one day. I thought of the whole world as nothing but a refulgent light of the complete soul of Allah. I believed that every moment, I was receiving the unfailing blessing of Allah. Again, I didn't think of anything happening without His will. But, one day, the proud head of this infallible victor bowed down. When the pain of my wounded body aggravated daily, my faith in Allah gradually got reduced in the same vogue. Then, I realized that killing brutally human beings in the name of Allah can never be the *Dharmayuddha* (the battle of righteousness). I was entering into the unfathomable mud of sinful acts unintentionally. I have no escape from that.
Tulasi :	At last, you understood your fault. For that, today, leaving the Muslim religion, you have accepted the rules and ideals of the Hindu religion.
Salabega :	I was strongly inclined and attached to the Hindu religion for some days. Still, I have not accepted the Hindu religion. Today, I feel that the Hindu religion, like the Muslim religion, is also narrow and

		limited. I don't want to confine myself to any particular religion and get suffocated. I like the free flow of pure air that can't be static anywhere. Do you know what that pure air is, *Maa*? That's, above all religions, the ultimate Human Truth.
Tulasi	:	Is this Human Truth not in the Hindu religion? The Hindu religion was established as the *Sanatan* Religion in the world because of its generosity and high-mindedness. You believe that an invisible spiritual soul strengthens the human mind firmly. You have realized that spiritual soul and the firmness of your mind through this Hindu religion. Is it false?
Salabega	:	For that, I am revolving around being stranded on the horns of a dilemma and with hesitations and conflicts. How can I deny you that I don't realize that Supreme Soul every moment? Then, is that soul confined only to the Hindu religion?
Tulasi	:	And then? What religion is better than the Hindu religion? Where can you realize the Divine Soul so closely?
Salabega	:	Leave it. I can't argue with you. I don't have the right to hurt you on your traditional belief system of religion. I will be absorbed in meditation once more. I need more philosophical knowledge. *Maa*, let me think silently for a while. I am moving towards that calm, serene, sublime Nature. [Exit]

Tulasi	:	Sitting like this and thinking unnecessarily, his mind won't work correctly! All these baseless arguments! (Disturbed, she is walking for a while. When she looked back suddenly, she saw Lalbega had reached. She is heavily surprised at his arrival.)
Lalbega	:	Are you afraid of seeing me? No need to fear.
Tulasi	:	One who has cut off the shackles of fear many days earlier won't be afraid of anyone.
Lalbega	:	Are you still arrogant? Is there an animal in this world that is not afraid of insolent Lalbega?
Tulasi	:	You should know that I don't fear death at all. Life for me is very trivial and insignificant.
Lalbega	:	Oh! Are you surrendering so easily?
Tulasi	:	There is no need for conflicts. Please tell me what you want.
Lalbega	:	I want Salabega! Where's Salabega?
Tulasi	:	Salabega is absorbed in meditation. No meeting is possible.
Lalbega	:	Meditation? You are making me laugh! Is Lalbega's son, Salabega absorbed in meditation today? Will that meditation be a barrier in the meeting between father and son? Ha...ha...ha...You know very well that Lalbega is the owner of unconquerable power. He has done what he wants to do in life. You have completely forgotten that you are talking

		to the insolent Subedar Lalbega. There won't be any loss if you forget. I have come here today to pardon you for all your faults.
Tulasi	:	I know that you are mad in your power. For that is this mockery.
Lalbega	:	I have been worshipping my power and my adventurous spirit forever. You have been acquainted with my passion and adventurous spirit earlier. You must still remember. One day, I was mad after your voluptuous beauty. I have conquered you forcefully. Because of my power, I have made every impossible possible. It's my pride and self-consolation. This adventurous spirit gives me the inspiration for a new life.
Tulasi	:	New life? I am condemning your new life a hundred times. But you remember, Lalbega! You are showing your pride in conquering my insignificant body. But beating over my mind was out of your control. You have seen the rights only in the earthly eyes.
Lalbega	:	Your argument is so strange. Can the rights be ever heavenly?
Tulasi	:	Certainly. But not before the heartless pirate like Lalbega, who is forever unintelligible to the concept of heavenly right. That's why you are only the servant to your strength and power. You need to understand what the heart is about.
Lalbega	:	Can you deny that I had not loved

		you and not given you my love and affection?
Tulasi	:	Love-affection? Are you not ashamed of using these holy words from your mouth? Yes, why will you feel? For you, righteous and unholy, vice and virtue are all equal. You can do all sorts of cruelties worldwide by your tendency and disposition. Being engrossed in wine and women day and night, you think that nobody else is happier than you. But, can you speak whether you have experienced the 'real peace'?
Lalbega	:	Yes, I experienced this when plunging into your beauty's fire like a blind insect.
Tulasi	:	That day has passed. Then, you are correct that you were a blind insect. You have not understood anything except the carnal desire for sex. To love was far from you to be conquered, the way an animal, out of fear, crept into the forest, having seen the hunter.
Lalbega	:	Had I not loved you?
Tulasi	:	Don't try to insult the word 'to love' so cruelly. Did you love me? How much time did you take to forget that love? The agonies of my heart I can't forget, the ruler! Can you remember how cruelly you had expelled me from your home? When the colour and scent of the green fresh Tulasi of those days got lost, and when she turned into a yellowish withered leave, in your mind was created

		an unending storm for the rhythm of the dance of a young, beautiful Zaib-un-Nisa. And I was-
Lalbega	:	You have answered your question splendidly. Why are you trying to extend one more stupid question towards me?
Tulasi	:	As humans age, their minds' colours fade, and they look pale and discoloured. Is this your humanity?
Lalbega	:	Humanity?
Tulasi	:	Yes...yes, humanity. From that, society has heard the sound of the footsteps of the Almighty.
Lalbega	:	Don't show your courage to pronounce the word "*Ishwar*" before me. I wouldn't say I like the word *Ishwar*. If you say something about "Allah", I may listen to you.
Tulasi	:	That right is also not yours. You are a sinner and an atheist. You don't have faith in any religion. What you are with is only bigotry and fanaticism. Instead of blessings from Allah, you have received a 'curse'. That's why you are always restless and agitated. Disobeying humanity, you have turned yourself into a beast.
Lalbega	:	I have already crossed the limits of my tolerance, Tulasi! You have been so adventurous, looking at the calm state of my mind. But, it's enough. Keep it in mind, I am Lalbega.
Tulasi	:	The swelled flood doesn't come daily to the river of life, *Subedar* (Ruler). One day,

		that torrent will convert itself into a grey desert. You will then realize how poor and helpless you are, like a dying bird. Again, then and there, your 'egotism' will start crying in distress. After that, the severe cyclonic storm will come from all directions. You will be lost like a dust particle in the darkness.
Lalbega	:	I have not come here to hear this great philosophy from you. I don't have any need from you. Tell me where Salabega is.
Salabega	:	(Entering) *Pita* (Father)! You are here? My *pranam* to you! I am very grateful that the dust of your feet (*pa*rent) has reached this pauper's hut.
Lalbega	:	Perhaps, I would not come. But, after the Fakir returned from this place hopelessly, I was forced to come.
Salabega	:	I had made it clear to Fakir, "Had this meeting with you not happened, it would instead have been encouraging for me".
Lalbega	:	Have I come to you with hopes and aspirations only to hear this? I felt hurt a lot unnecessarily. Can't you understand the eagerness of a father's heart for his son?
Salabega	:	Where was your anxiety for so many days? Having shown your extreme paternal love, you expelled me from your home that day when I was at a very critical stage. You are unable to remember me for so long. Have you ever wanted to know

		whether Salabega is alive or dead? Why have you come today?
Lalbega	:	Salabega, you forget the past. You come with me. I repent for what I did in the past. I have come here to take you back.
Tulasi	:	You don't have the legal right to take him back with you. Salabega is my son. I have brought him back from the deathbed. In his heart, deserts are seen as the sea waves today. He is on the way to righteousness after leaving the world's life path. By God's grace, the blemishes of the murderer are no more with him. The whole world is pleased with his poetic soft resonance.
Lalbega	:	I'm well aware of your evil plan, Tulasi. You are trying to play with fire, taking advantage of Salabega's illness and your flight from home. Keeping him with you, you have made him a *kafir*. (Atheist). But it takes more efforts to avoid my blood. You will see how your bridge of hopes will vanish within a second.
Salabega	:	You are my father. Please don't insult my mother like this. A fire is still burning in my heart. My name could have been lost many days ago if I had not sheltered with my mother.
Lalbega	:	Believe me, Salabega! That day, in an inauspicious moment, I suddenly disregarded you. But, for that, I have suffered mentally a lot. Perhaps, you can't realize that. Salabega is my brave

		son! His stay can't be under a tree. He can stay in the palace. For that, only with the love and attachment of a father, I have come to you.
Tulasi	:	I have understood why there is this stir of compassion in a father's heart. Where was your love and attachment the day you expelled Salabega from your palace? You had done this only, for he was a barrier to you and a hideous sight in your entertainment hall. He was unbearable to the beautiful dancer Zaib-un-Nisa. At that time, you didn't show any love for your son. There was no hesitation in your mind to send your son to bed of death. As he has completely recovered today from illness and regained his earlier power, you have your love for him. Hasn't it come out suddenly?
Lalbega	:	Well, you can speak high of yourself. It's my bad fortune to hear all these words. I have made you a queen from a beggar one day. That's why you are with so much pride. You can show your gratefulness very well! You perhaps don't know it's a sin to touch the shadow of a *kafir* (Non-Muslim) woman like you. Because of that sin today, I am forced to tolerate the abuses and disrespects from an ordinary woman like you. This is only for Salabega's respect.
Salabega	:	Please remember that she is my mother. She is in flesh and blood and a mother

		of all sorts of compassion. I can't tolerate her being insulted before me.
Lalbega	:	I am not insulting you. I have much respect for you.
Tulasi	:	It's natural to honour and respect him because you have thought; he is well and in good health now. Again, as earlier, he will plunder wealth for you. He can add fuel to your enjoyment. Your paternal love is the other name of self-gratification. Had you not been with that, why would you have come here?
Lalbega	:	Are you not hesitant to speak these sinful words in your mouth? How can you pollute so badly the holy father-son relationship? You are blamed!
Tulasi	:	Today, I can see your judgment very well between vice and virtue. I am virtuous and blessed. But remember, having been released from hell, Salabega is now on the path of righteousness towards the heavenly kingdom. He can never return to his earlier past.
Lalbega	:	This is only the voice of the weak and the frail. Salabega has built himself up to my ideals. Today, he may temporarily have some aversion and indifference in his heart for the past. But, he can make that heart as strong as the thunder and indifferent as the sea.
Salabega	:	But, Today, I have become fragile. It's true that one day, I was trying to be a bold pirate by your command. Then I

		promised to raise bloody wars against the poor innocent people throughout life and ruin Hindu Gods and Goddesses in temples. After that, I considered that killing the Hindus was my religion. In my heart, there was not a single drop of compassion for anybody. That bloodthirstiness and that inhumanity are the causes of my downfall and degradation. When I have not developed any sympathy for anybody, who will smear and anoint a colour of compassion upon my heart for any reason?
Lalbega	:	The whole world may be disinterested in showing a pinch of sympathy towards you, but I can show you that as your father.
Salabega	:	No...! That sympathy is associated with self-interest because there are many expectations, no heart, and no truth.
Lalbega	:	These are the incoherent words of a lunatic. Past has gone! That past has already been drowned in the lethal automation of time. Now, you prepare yourself as a perfect son to a father! I hope you won't at least be disobedient to me!
Tulasi	:	I want to ask, "On what right have you come here to take Salabega with you?"
Lalbega	:	Perhaps, Salabega can make you better understand than me what right is.
Salabega	:	Oh...! Why is this conflict? I don't want to be indulged in this conflict. Having been

overloaded with all the world's curses, on what inauspicious moment was I born on this dusky earth? I couldn't make my parents console and smile. No, I have decided now my duties. Not, at all. Maa! Can't you forgive your disobedient son? I can't stay here for a moment. I leave you both, since my journey is different.

Lalbega : This is the right answer from the mouth of the brave son of Lalbega. Ha...ha... ha...! (Laughing)

Tulasi : (Her eyes widen out of surprise.) How could you hurt me so severely, Salabega? Don't you have a heart? (Silent) Yes, you go, my son- stay peacefully. Though I have nurtured you, I could not keep you with me. Being disobedient to my hundred requests, you had become an inhuman. Now, towards the last stage of my life, I got you for some days. You returned to me as a human being. My heart was filled with happiness every moment to take care of you. But don't I have that energy to keep you with me? Be happy, my son- That's my peace, that's my contentment. Looking at the empty sky, this unfortunate mother will stay under this tree. She will be happy imagining your wealth and prosperity. [Eyes are full of tears.]

Lalbega : You should, at least, know that Salabega is not a coward who will stay concealing his face in his mother's lap for long.

Salabega	:	You will forgive me, *Pita* (Father)! I am also not accompanying you to your place. I have already made it clear that my journey is different.
Lalbega	:	Are you mocking at me, Salabega?
Salabega	:	No, I don't have that kind of arrogance. One day, I saw the sphere or brightness of light lost from the sun. The sun has become a useless object like an iron sphere which can't give light, can't give life, can't give beauty, and can't give happiness. But today, that sun shines brightly before my eyes, dispelling all the mist. I can't enter again that darkness and that haziness.
Lalbega	:	Make it clear, Salabega! What do you want? There are two ways for you: One is of wealth and prosperity, and the other is of danger and poverty.
Salabega	:	I am not ready to accept any one of the two. I don't have any scope to love, especially one particular religion. For me, both Hindu and Muslim religions are equal. The narrow-mindedness of the faith has made man heartless. Again, this has made man out of the path of humanity. But today, I am above this narrow parochialism. I am neither a Hindu nor a Muslim.
Tulasi	:	You are the son of a Hindu mother. You are Hindu! You are the supreme devotee of Lord Jagannath.
Salabega	:	No, You are the son of Muslim father–

		You are a Muslim! You have strong faith in Allah.
Salabega	:	You don't try to pull me into the darkness of falsehood. I know, you are blind to see any other religion except your own. Both of you are of this fanaticism. In the name of religion, you have genuinely kicked the 'Real Divine Soul'. Before me, Mecca is false; before me, Puri is false.
Lalbega	:	No, Mecca can't be false. Don't show your arrogance to deny the holy land of Prophet Muhammad.
Salabega	:	I have no faith in Allah. I don't accept the Muslim religion. The religion that has not given me the eternal touch of humanity, and where there is no hesitation for bloodshed in the name of religion, has been given up by me forever.
Tulasi	:	But, Hindu religion. Your adorable God, Jagannath, has directed you on the path of humanity. Can you deny this?
Salabega	:	Yes, I can. You know that I have developed a deep love for the Hindu religion. But, when I saw the Hindu religion closely, I acquired no confidence in the Hindu religion. The Hindu religion is also not free from narrow parochialism. It's also not free from violence, malice and enmity. Tell- You tell, *Maa*- Is your Salabega telling lies?
Tulasi	:	(Silent)
Salabega	:	Why are you silent? I know that you don't have any answer to this question. One

		day, I had strong faith and conviction for the Hindu religion and Lord Jagannath. But I don't have it right now. If the caste system of the Hindu religion is created from the works and conduct, why can't I become a Brahman? Why was the principal door of the fallen and the sinful (*Patitapabana*) closed for me? Why did I remain as a mean *jaban* (a foreigner or a non-Hindu) forever? From this vile *jaban* stage, I have put aside all kinds of narrow parochialism. I have now been consecrated to the great, generous human religion. Can you realize?
Lalbega and Tulasi	: :	Salabega! Salabega!
Salabega	:	After a long time, my delusion gets cleared. I have explored the 'Truth'. In my heart's neat and clean sky is the flood of moonlit night today. I will march ahead, overcoming all falsehood and inhumanities. Truth shines brightly before me like a paddy crop in the golden sunlight. Today onwards Salabega will start his new expedition. That expedition is for the 'Great Truth' and the holy touch of the 'Divine Soul'. Please, don't stop me anymore. My path is clearly defined and decided. O, my father and mother, my creators! At the time of my departure, I see your faces glistening with happiness.

Please don't curse me. Bless me! Bless me- I will be capable of preaching the everlasting Human religion.

[Salabega leaves the place, touching the feet of his parents. In his face glows a beautiful light of hope and exploration. Lalbega and Tulasi are stupefied and looking at Salabega's path.]

****

COLUMBUS

DRAMATIS PERSONAE

Play Columbus

Major Characters
Columbus
Ferdinand
Isabella
Roldan
Boyle
Bartholomew
Diego
Pynchon
Acquaday
Minor Characters
Teacher, three male students and one female student
Two Navigators

SCENE-I

Teacher	: (Striking the table) Stop talking now. Shut up. If you don't listen to the lectures of Geography-
First Student	: We are not interested, Sir-
Second Student	: We are hungry, Sir-
Third Class	: We have already attended six classes, Sir-
First Student	: Our mind doesn't receive now-
Teacher	: Still, you have to attend the classes mindfully. Otherwise, you will face problems later! From the outset I tell you that you can't understand everything, while studying at your level.
Girl Student	: (in a low voice) Sir does not respect our feelings. He never understands us.
Third Student	: Shut up!
Teacher	: The Geography course doesn't show any sympathy to anyone. It's tough, challenging and full of dry information. The element that transposes an individual in mind and soul doesn't come to its domain. But are all portions of Geography equal? As usual, it is practised from the beginning. Today's

topic is about historical geography. This geography is kind and approachable. It's too cruel and brutal. This map will guide you regarding its status and territorial explanation. The map is not only a collection of lifeless lines. Sometimes, these lines become very strong and lively. Can you imagine how romantic they can be? (Silence for a while) You must have some knowledge regarding Christopher Columbus's adventurous sea voyage. Have you ever thought of it? Like his sea voyage, his life journey is extraordinary and dramatic.

First Student : Then the Geography course would have been drama!

Teacher : Yes, it's play! See whether it's play or not. O, Isabella, come here. Come. Why are you sitting?

Girl Student : Are you telling me? Me?

Teacher : Yes, you. Now onwards you consider yourself as The Great Empress of Spain, Isabella. Well, please be seated in this chair. Let's think this is not a chair but a throne. No, no, the way you are sitting needs to be corrected. Pose yourself in queen's style. Why are you laughing? It's not right. Be serious and show solemnity in your style of sitting. More powerful and dignified! Now you come, Ferdinand! Yes, be seated in the chair at this side. Let your royal style be observed in your class. Your solemnity misses in your attitude. Columbus—Christopher Columbus—you can stand in front of them. Cross your fingers at the back. You are now standing imprisoned in the Royal Court of Spain. The court is in session to give the final verdict regarding your case/decision. Well, don't keep your head erect. Keep your face downward, as if you were overwhelmed by the pains and humiliations you received from others. (Silence) The court is about to start. The singers start singing in chorus about the King's greatness and generosity.

All : (with clapping)
In the world, there is no country like Spain,
It's fortified with green fields, trees and creepers.
Truth, Righteousness and Justice are ever found,
O Brother! We are great and happy here to take birth.
Our Kings and Queens are not comparable to anybody,
The world brightens, listening to its monumental stories.

Roldan : Let there be a victory for the Great Emperor Ferdinand and the Great Empress Isabella! As per the direction of the Emperor and the Empress, I now present issues brought against the royal traitor:
Issue number one is that, by birth, Columbus is from Italy, and he does not show any interest sincerely for the territorial expansion of Spain. Now, he is the ruler of the western Indian isles he has explored and wants to enjoy as an independent leader. His son and

	brother are deployed in different newly discovered lands for their governance. He has plundered the gold treasures collected from those isles.
Ferdinand	: Columbus, how could you at last betray Spain? I had never thought of it, even in a dream. When you were roaming here and there, like a lunatic in different countries, nobody paid any attention to your proposal. Can you remember that stage you have already undergone? At that time, who was coming forward to help you?
Boyle	: Strong betrayal, My Lord! No forgiveness for this heinous crime! Lord Jesus will be unhappy if a sinful person like him is pardoned or forgiven.
Ferdinand	: That day, most of the councilors tabled a common resolution- spending a lot of money on such a voyage is a matter of lacking foresight. I also displayed my displeasure and hesitation to your proposal. But, when the Great Queen Isabella agreed to sell her costly ornaments and consented with an approving nod for the sea voyage for expenditures, I was compelled to sanction the approved amount from the Royal treasury.
Roldan	: At that time, the Royal Treasury was experiencing a financial crunch because of our continuous war with the Moors.
Isabella	: Past is no more. We won't gain anything if we discuss unnecessarily the past. Who

knows that a smoky, poisonous layer of treachery will suffocate that day's strong avidity and excitement? The person whom the people treated as a lunatic appealed to me a lot. I was pleased with his strong determination and iron will for stability. I had been inclined and poured my heart and soul into the Grand National deed.

Boyle : Ah! I am entirely disappointed. My heart is full of contempt for this type of spirited man. Very strange! This is a magician's illusion. Being trapped in it for a while, the Emperor and the Empress opened their hearts sympathetically to this mean person.

Ferdinand : Now I realize all the councillors are deeply annoyed. What could I have done at that moment? I lost my conscience and intelligence at the magical tricks of a traitor. Showering the prestige on an undeserving candidate, I strongly repent today. (Silence) All right, Roldan! Place before us the next issue-

Roldan : The Spaniards who had travelled with him are oppressed and subdued. Again, he exploited the innocent natives of the Isles inexpressively and sent them to Europe as enslaved people.

Boyle : None of these allegations is false, Emperor! As Roldan himself is a lawyer, there is no question of making any false statement. Besides, Commander Margaret is an

	eye-witness of all these and a religious bishop like me. The royal member of the court Acquaday, sent from the court, has investigated all the accusations raised against him.
Roldan	: Again, Baron Bobadilla, having studied the detailed report on the spot, without any bias, declared him the culprit and made him present before the Royal Court as a prisoner. The Great Emperor! You give a final verdict on this matter to know whether there is any difference between my allegations and Bishop Boyle's.
Ferdinand	: Now I realize how we get entangled in danger if we take any vital decision without investigating the pros and cons of the matter. Today, I am ashamed of expressing myself before the committee members. I was very emotional at that time. The expansion of the Spanish empire overseas, storing gold wealth and preaching Christianity were the dreams that clouded me. Otherwise, I was not ready at all to spend a lot.
Isabella	: I am not disturbed by this tremendous financial loss. But, I am rather profoundly touched and moved by his sending the innocent natives of the Isles to Europe as enslaved people. I am a strong dissenter of the heinous system. That means I am also indirectly responsible for this.
Ferdinand	: Columbus, you were simply a sailor. I made all kinds of arrangements for you,

	having observed your extraordinary adventurous spirit for exploring new lands. Is this the reward for the help I extended to you?
Boyle	: Let ungrateful Columbus suffer severely for not preserving religion and improving the country, Emperor!
Roldan	: On behalf of the barons of the court, I also request you the same.
Ferdinand	: Columbus, after hearing the opinions of the esteemed court members, I will punish you abruptly. I am also allowing you to defend yourself against the allegations raised. Now, you speak whether the allegations made against you are true or false.
Columbus	: I am grateful to you for your generosity. I have heard all the accusations, from the Great Emperor and Empress to the committee members. I thought that I would not respond at all. I will accept the Capital Punishment in silence. But when you have allowed me to speak sympathetically-
Boyle	: This is the holy Royal Court. But, here, no false arguments are tolerated.
Columbus	: While smiling, Columbus can accept the Capital Punishment. He will never propagate any false statement. How do you think the person who has deteriorated his mind and body lifelong to discovering the Truth will tell lies today? (Boyle tries to obstruct him.)

Ferdinand	: Boyle, Let Columbus speak!
Columbus	: The Great Emperor and the Great Empress! Both of you have shown your sympathy incessantly. I am grateful to you forever. I will never forget your contributions once I last breathe for the heavenly abode. However, in this court, I have been described as a stern traitor and very ungrateful in my heart and soul. Can you imagine how that has touched me?
Ferdinand	: Please reply only to the allegations made against you!
Columbus	: From the very beginning, I told you that I aim to enhance the pride of Spain. I have yet to be strayed and diverted from that objective to date. My motherland is indeed Italy, but my workplace is Spain. My identity in Italy is just the son of a weaver. But, my identity in Spain is the 'The Emperor of the Ocean'. For which country is this identity possible for me? Now, you all speak to whom I should be more attached: one mother has completed her responsibility after giving birth to a child. Another mother has nurtured the child and helped him grow into a complete man and fulfill all his extreme desires. You believe me, please. I have loved Spain from my heart and soul. My only ambition is to amass its wealth. There is no question of non-nationality/non-nationalism in it.

Ferdinand	: Following your treaty, the countries you have discovered are now under the Spanish Empire. But, you have been deployed to rule and govern those countries as a royal representative of the court. However, you have not been given the right to establish them as independent states and consider yourself the independent ruler.
Columbus	: The allegation is entirely false and the plotted conspiracy of some of the persons who are very selfish in their approach against me. I promise I have never chalked out this plan in my mind.
Ferdinand	: You said, "In this expedition, the huge expenditures Spain will do, many times of that you will bring back the wealth from those explored countries." As you told me, the amount of gold wealth you handed us is much less. There is a wide gap between what you say and what you do.
Roldan	: Is there any proof that you have not hoarded more gold wealth under your possession?
Columbus	: I can confirm no evidence of this baseless allegation. I imagined before the sea voyage that gold pieces must have been dispersed widely in different parts of the Eastern countries. But in reality, that was not seen. You can ask my co-travelers and inquire into the fact. It is true that until now, I have not gathered gold wealth

	as per our expectation, but I have yet to withdraw myself from this arduous task! Then, is territorial expansion not better than the accumulation of gold? In my third expedition, I discovered the long-stretched coastal areas of South America.
Isabella	: That was discovered earlier by the navigator Amerigo Vespucci one year back.
Columbus	: Amerigo Vespucci was a real Tartuffe and shrewd preacher. How far is it possible for a ship-loading contractor? After getting information from my sailors, he has falsely spread everywhere that he is the explorer of America. It's my sorrow and obsession. Nobody investigated the facts. The vast land was named after a swindler. The real explorer's name came to the limelight only for a while. What else can be more cheating than this? I am still bearing this shock; of whose hopes, of whose supports?
Boyle	: But, you are much interested in the colonial expansion and the hoarding of gold. As a result, you have relegated to the backdrop and neglected enormously the teaching and preaching of Jesus Christ, the savior of humanity. There is nothing more heinous crime than this.
Columbus	: This may be a pardonable crime. But Lord Jesus can speak the words of my heart and soul, how I have not been able to execute my responsibilities in extreme

Salabega and Columbus | 73

	circumstances. Despite my hectic schedule, I have also established some churches. After colonial establishment, I had, of course, planned to establish religion.
Ferdinand	: You appointed your sons and brothers in governmental works of different regions. How far is it legal?
Columbus	: You are unaware of my critical situation in the distanced colonies. Emperor! The employees and officials under my supervision have frequently deceived and plotted conspiracies against me. Because of that, I did not consider them responsible persons. That's why the relatives-
Isabella	: This argument is feeble. This kind of nepotism and narrow parochialism is unacceptable for a great person like you.
Columbus	: For this, I am ashamed of, Empress! Keeping in view the precise pressure, I couldn't find any other option except-
Ferdinand	: Then, why are the innocent natives of the Isles exploited and sent to Europe as enslaved people? Can I know what sort of detailed pressure you were with?
Columbus	: Neither I nor my representatives have exploited and subdued the poor natives. In the places where the inhabitants are not accepting our obedience and governance, not cooperating, and revolting against the system, we have tried to dominate them. As stated, some dissenters and agitators,

	the Caribs (Cannibals), who are fond of having human flesh, are sent as enslaved people.
Isabella	: You know that I strongly contempt the system of slavery. As a representative of our court, you have executed that system. It's regrettable. You are unable to realize this. For this, I am getting humiliated.
Columbus	: I accept my crimes. I am very sorry to disobey your order and respect, Empress! I confess and humbly surrender before the court to pardon me for this.
Roldan	: Columbus has stated herewith his counter-arguments unnecessarily to set himself off allegations filed against him. Again, on the whole, he has confessed his crimes. It will be deplorable for us if he gets released without Punishment for the crimes he had committed earlier. The common opinion of the barons present here for Columbus is Capital Punishment.
Boyle	: I wholeheartedly support this proposal. The Emperor and the Empress are the representatives of Lord Jesus, the most benevolent. In their choice, if Columbus is not punished, there will be obstacles to establishing religion.
Columbus	: Columbus had not argued for his release from the Capital Punishment, Boyle. All of you are mistaken. He is prepared to accept whatever the severity of Capital Punishment.
Ferdinand	: If you are sentenced to death-

Columbus	: For that, I will never retreat, Emperor! One who has fought with death every day, why will that person be afraid of it? (Pause) What I have chosen as my mode of life and vow is constantly encountering a vile form of death at every step. Indirectly, I have won over the other world (Death) in my expedition, along with the darkness of ignorance. That's my solace and bright consolation. I am divinely blessed to vanquish natural death. So, how can I be afraid of this human decision, Emperor?
Ferdinand	: You are, of course, not being given any capital punishment. Still, for the respect of the court-
Columbus	: I have expressed my views clearly. Why are you insulting repeatedly by spelling out the rules of punishment? As you have already decided to punish, you should punish now, but to whom? Will you punish the ghost of Columbus? You have already killed Columbus. Columbus, who had traversed the deep, dangerous Atlantic Ocean, declared before the world that the earth was spherical and rounded. Travelling the ocean westward, one can reach the East. The stories of water giants and hell are false. That 'The Emperor of the Ocean' is already dead, not bearing the burden of deception and disgrace in the Court of Spain.
Isabella	: Columbus!
Columbus	: To follow the Truth is very menacing and

	life-threatening, Empress! The shortage of people in this world can bear the Truth. Those people who are here to discover the Truth only die forcibly. And I am-
Isabella	: You can speak what you want freely and fearlessly.
Columbus	: You must have marked since the day I had started my sea voyage, the fire of jealousy rose in the mind of the councilors. They have been trying to humiliate me most of the time. At last, both of you are also trapped by nets of conspiracy they have set. What else can be more disastrous than to watch this? (Silent) How could you forget that day of the past so early? The day Columbus returned to explore the New Land with your blessings of infinite love and compassion, the entire Europe was astonished and looked at the Spanish Empire anxiously. The Emperor of England, Henry VII, pronounced publicly for me a new coinage, 'The Emperor of the Ocean'. You have also greeted me with the phrase the 'Great Lord Don Christopher Columbus' in the Royal court of Barcelona. Can you speak about why you did honour me that day? Is it for my patriotism, disloyalty, and betrayal of the country/ terrorism? (Silence) Columbus, who established the pride of Spain in the entire world, is standing now helplessly before the court as a general culprit. This is what

	the mockery of history is. (Silence) I only want to die to save myself from this extremely shameful situation. With folded palms, I humbly pray before you to punish me with the 'death sentence', the Great Empress.
Isabella	: (Descending from the throne) You are great, Columbus! You are great! I am setting you free from the shackles in my own hands. (Silence) We have understood you wrong. You pardon us, Columbus! (You are released and accessible now.)
Columbus	: I have been pleased with your behaviour, Great Empress! How can I convey my gratitude to you?
Isabella	: I have respected your adventurous spirit forever, Columbus! Today, credit goes to you with the same amount of love and affection. If you have any desire for the next sea voyage-
Ferdinand	: Yes, you are permitted to go on your next expedition and to discover new lands afresh. Let the pride of Spain be enhanced.
Columbus	: What sea voyage will I do now? I have reached the first step of my old age. Still then, if the Great Emperor and Empress desire-

SCENE-II

Teacher	: Columbus started another sea voyage, the last expedition of his life. What was the consequence? It's whether victory or defeat?
First Student	: Can a brave explorer be defeated?
Teacher	: It's 09 May 1502. Columbus went on an expedition, loading four ships of food materials. His brother Bartholomew and his second son Ferdinand accompanied him.
Second Student	: Where did they reach this time, Sir?
Teacher	: They reached the Panama Coast. From this place, he tried very hard to cross the other side of the sea. He had the idea that on the other side of it was his most desired 'Land of Gold', India. But, he was miserable to cross the sea. Despite his hard effort, he didn't come across any strait.
Third Student	: Then?
Teacher	: Moving to the west, he reached the Coast of Mexico. He set up immediately the colonies in that vast land. But-

Teacher	: The native inhabitants of that land vehemently opposed and assaulted Columbus. By then, they had already been aware of the cruel exploitation of the White Government's policy.
Girl Student	: There must have been a loss of life and wealth.
Teacher	: Despite the use of guns, bullets, and explosives, he could not counter-attack and overcome their strong, wild prowess. Columbus, who has won over Nature, for the first time here, got vanquished.
Girl Student	: Oh, what a tragedy of life!
Teacher	: With this, his day of suffering didn't end. While leaving the place out of fear, he faced a natural calamity. Because of the severe cyclonic storm, he lost two of his ships. With the other two ships, he reached the Jamaica Island.
First Student	: For God's sake, he saved his life. He must have taken rest peacefully as the survivor.
Teacher	: No, the people of Jamaica vehemently hated the foreigners from the beginning. To know whether the situation was favourable, Columbus sent some navigators to Santo Domingo.
Second Student	: Was there any assistance?
Teacher	: He didn't get any help for eight months. He could have sent somebody to Hispaniola. But there was also a severe shortage of food. On the other hand, the food materials stored on the ship were about to finish. All the crew members

	and the navigators needed food, and sometimes they stayed half-starved. The situation forces him to return to Spain.
Girl student	: Alas! Was there a horrible consequence? His physical courage ended along with his moral courage.
Teacher	: Is it possible to describe before you the mental state of Columbus while experiencing the last stage of his life? We need to act on this. Acting!
Girl Student	: Again acting?
Teacher	: Yes, here is the invincible Columbus's last stage of life! The old and weak Columbus is on his deathbed. Beside his bed are his brother Bartholomew and his son Diego. (The slow music of sorrowful moment)
Columbus	: Bartholomew and Diego! Are you all with me?
Bartholomew	: Yah, Brother! Here we are sitting beside you.
Columbus	: I can't see anything correctly, Bartholomew. Everything seems to be dusky. The eyes that helped me witness in the great ocean for miles and miles disowned me at last. (Silence) Yes, all left me one by one. I am alone on the lonely sea beach. In everybody's face for me lie contempt and disobedience. Mostly, I look at the infinite sky like a helpless child. The atmosphere is serene and static. Columbus has returned from the expedition, but there is no welcome ceremony.
Bartholomew	: Who could have welcomed you? Your

	most loved well-wisher, Empress Isabella, has already passed away. The Emperor Ferdinand is indifferent about you. He has forgotten you completely.
Columbus	: To me? Has he forgotten me? Has the Emperor forgotten the person who had expanded his empire many times more than the original at the cost of his own life? Is it so? Yes, yes, it's natural to forget. The reason is simple: I was helpful to him at this moment. Finally, I came back empty-handed with the unpleasant experience of defeat.
Diego	: How will you benefit from recollecting all those memories?
Columbus	: Yes, yes. Since that day, I was deprived of. The Nature upon which I was a winner now threatens me and takes revenge. That separated me and left me alone forever. At last, it took more work for me to collect a palm of rice daily.
Diego	: Those who have sacrificed their lives for the country always struggle with want and poverty as friends in daily life.
Columbus	: Having seen the deadly appearance of poverty, I would not have been heartbroken, had I been shown respect and approved of my achievements. But while I am roaming in the road as a homeless pauper because of starvation, people are poking fun at me. Thinking of me as a lunatic, they are running after me. They have ridiculed me. How ungrateful

		and heartless the earth is!
Bartholomew	:	That's what the fate is. The earth that had crowned you one day rejected and threw you as a useless flower in due course of events!
Columbus	:	Bartholomew! Please think of the day when I had left the coast of Mexico and fought with the tornado, the massive storm. Had I lost my candle of life that day? That death could have been better and happier! I could feel that the end was nearing step by step. I would have lost my life while hearing the echoes of vast sea waves! I would have realized in intense excitement that I had embraced death. So hot is that touch. Ah-
Bartholomew	:	Try to sleep, my brother. At this stage, we are so excited-
Columbus	:	Dangerous? Isn't it? What else will we have to lose, Bartholomew? What's with me except this useless, helpless life? At this moment, if I passed away, nobody would show his sympathy. Why will they say? My death won't make any tragedy today, Bartholomew. I will experience the end, not of 'the Emperor of Ocean' but of a beggar, Columbus.
Diego	:	Please stop all this, Baba. You will recover completely within one or two days. I pray before God.
Columbus	:	I don't have to wait for one or two days, my son, but only for a while. Now, death approaches slowly. I realize, it is tricky,

	but it is so cold and chilly. Where is the warmth of that day? (He sleeps for a while.)
Bartholomew	: Perhaps he has slept.
Columbus	: (He started shouting suddenly.) Bartholomew! Where are you? Are you with me?
Bartholomew	: We are here.
Columbus	: The death of Victor Columbus is not so easy, Bartholomew! Do you think that I am defeated? What's this? What are you saying? As a defeated warrior, am I retreating myself from the battlefield? No, impossible! to beat is never scripted in the horoscope of the hero. Of my helpless condition, others may think that I am defeated. But how can I think of it? I have never thought of being overpowered at any time. (Silence) the most loved brother Bartholomew! My co-traveler and the friend of victory, Bartholomew! Can you help me hear the story of my victorious expedition before I breathe last? If I enter the other world (unseen world of death) enjoying the best experiences and excitements of my earlier victory-
	[The screen is changed. The ocean starts roaring. The mixed chaotic clamour of cry and happiness is heard from a distance. Along with that, the ringing of the bell/ gong hung on the top of Saint George Church is also heard.]
Columbus	: Brethren! It is the auspicious moment of 03

August 1492. He started a revolutionary expedition. We will reach the East having navigated westward. That's what has not been conceived in anybody's mind. We will turn this into a reality. (Silence) See here the highest point of the church. Saint George looks at us eagerly. The ringing bell of the church stirs excitement within us, and we are mad now. In this sound are reverberated the blessings of Messiah, Lord Jesus. Have faith in God, the Almighty. We will certainly win. See again how the Morning Star brightens and signs positively for our victory. (The ship puffs her sail.)

Navigator I : How many days will we take, Admiral?

Columbus : Probably one month or a few more days than one month.

Navigator I : I am terrified of whether we will touch the new land.

Columbus : Why do these perplexed thoughts come to your mind, Joseph?

Navigator I : Not only to my mind but to all the minds here, Sir. Because of the King's order, all are forced to come. Otherwise, there is no peace in anybody's mind. All of us are horrified. At any moment, we may lose our life in the great ocean.

Navigator II : We were all interested in staying at home. At the time of departure, my wife and son were crying wholeheartedly. When I think of it, I am overwhelmed. Are we going to return alive?

Navigator I	: The same situation is with everybody, Admiral. Now before me are the tearful eyes of my parents, brother and sister, wife and children.
Columbus	: You must remove all these emotions from your mind, Joseph. Our sea voyage is difficult and inaccessible. Being a son of the sea, it's shameful if we are afraid of the sea.
Navigator II	: We don't have the fear of the sea voyage. To run after an impossible is highly dangerous.
Columbus	: What's impossible? We have to make the impossible possible.
Navigator II	: Had the impossible been made possible, why would others not have traversed the Atlantic Ocean so far?
Columbus	: If we repeat what others have done, where will be our quality and specific honour of identity? Try to observe the form and nature of the impossible. Feel the excitement of converting the impossible possible. Don't allow your life to run so smoothly and comfortably.
Navigator I	: Everybody wants a simple lifestyle. Who wants to struggle in life?
Columbus	: If you don't struggle, life has no happiness. Is life a life without stir and excitement? There is rise and fall and victory and defeat in life. Life becomes more romantic and enthusiastic at that moment when we try to live in the light and darkness of hope and disappointment.

Navigator I	: Will all look for this?
Columbus	: It's not right that others don't want and we won't. Our life is of different elements that are not with others. We have come to this world to work hard. Our happiness lies in the unattainable success. If we succeed with a lot of difficulty, there is our happiness.
Navigator II	: (Taking a long breath) Where is our happiness? Suffering is the only friend of our life. For such a long sea voyage, you can't think of the mental state of our ordinary navigators, Admiral.
Columbus	: I can feel your sorrow. Am I not a man of flesh and blood? I know the complex life we have undertaken, leaving behind our family members. But what will we do? We have also a responsibility for our country. You may think that I am thrilled. Time and again, I also remember my motherless son. At that moment, I feel that my blood gets coagulated. But we have to suppress all our sorrows in hearts. These days will pass on. Then, there will come the most desired moment of victory. Can you imagine when we will return to our country with immense pride of accomplishment for exploring the 'New Land'? The happiness in the minds of family members will be more intense than the happiness in the country people when we reach our land.

SCENE-III

Navigator I	: How many days have we stayed afloat in this great ocean?
Navigator II	: I am unable to recognize? A single day is a month here. When the day ends and the night approaches-
Navigator I	: We will go on floating forever. We are still determining where we will reach. When will we reach?
Navigator II	: Yes, we will reach. Why won't we get it? One day, we will surely reach the palace of the sea monsters or the hell. Who knows, the path of the ocean is infinitely extended to that place?
Navigator I	: When I think of it, my body trembles in fear, O my brother! But Columbus says that the stories of the sea monsters or the hell are entirely false. It's a superstition.
Navigator II	: You have also been mad listening to this mad person. We can't say anything because of the King's decree. We work like a machine. Otherwise-
Navigator I	: So strange! How did our King hear his

	words? Considering him a lunatic, all others had been driven away.
Navigator II	: Has he travelled the countries without food and water? He was disappointed by Portugal, Genoa and Venice-
Navigator I	: Our Empress was very anxious. He convinced her tactfully-
Navigator II	: Running after an uncertainty / a mirage will undoubtedly lead a country to a significant expenditure.
Navigator I	: Not only that? The Emperor agrees to all his conditions. The number of countries Columbus will discover will be taken care of by him as a royal representative of the court. He will also be the Commander-in-Chief of the Navy. He will also take one-tenth of the Gold Wealth he will bring to the country.
Navigator II	: Truly, Columbus is mad. Perhaps the King is also mad like him. Who gets agreed to all the conditions?
Navigator I	: All the people of the Royal Court ridiculed and mocked him scornfully and said-Yesterday's pauper of the road wants to become the Emperor at once. Who can give this proposal, unless he is mad?
Navigator II	: Leave this, Brother! If we think of that, we can also be mad. Now, we float in the unfathomable sea at this madman's knowledge, forgetting our life.
Navigator I	: We can't calculate the distance we have covered so far in the ocean. If we float, we will reach the endpoint of the sea and

	lose ourselves in the fathomless depth of the great ocean.
Navigator II	: Columbus says, "The Earth is not flat like paper, but rounded like an orange."
Navigator I	: Rounded? Then, on the top plane, we are walking on foot. But the people on the bottom plane may need to walk. Will they walk on head, taking their legs up?
Navigator II	: O, you can see, see now. The mast of the Pinta ship is inclined to one side. The ship swims like a tortoise.
Navigator I	: Shut up! If it breaks down, it will be better. The transatlantic voyage of Columbus will end here. So, we will return home to see our children and wife. We will be safe because of the Lord Jesus.
Navigator II	: Wonderful!
Navigator I	: No need to be worried. I know, the mast has been loosely installed. In the ship factory, some of us have done this. Everybody is afraid of life. Convincing and controlling this obstinate Columbus will be challenging if some mishap does not happen.

SCENE-IV

Columbus	: (Shouting) Captain Pynchon, Captain Pynchon, the mast of your ship is, perhaps, tilted or broken.
Pynchon	: Yes, yes, I know. Our mechanics are working day and night. There is no improvement. The mast is yet to be fixed correctly.
Columbus	: Then?
Pynchon	: What's the other alternative? I can't see anything except returning to Palos.
Columbus	: Return? Is it so? Can we show our face in Spain?
Pynchon	: Who can control the natural calamities?
Columbus	: I have never expected to hear the words of defeat from your mouth, Pynchon!
Pynchon	: Please, you say, "What can be done at this critical juncture of time?"
Columbus	: Don't worry. If we travel southward from here, we will reach the Canary Islands. We will repair our ship there and again move westward. In the meantime, we will load vegetables, water tanks, and fuel wood on our ship.

SCENE-V

Columbus	:	Captain Pynchon! We have already travelled a long distance after leaving the Canary Islands. There's no fear. The conspiracy of the Portugal King is in vain.
Pynchon	:	Anyway, the storm helps us move forward. All three ships are travelling at three times more speed than the original. Santa Maria is also moving parallelly with Pinta.
Columbus	:	We are with the blessings of Lord Jesus, our Saviour. What's fear?
Pynchon	:	I was worried when we got the information from that foreign ship that the King of Portugal sent a warrior ship to get hold of you.
Columbus	:	Having seen this storm, they have returned.
Pynchon	:	They can't see our ships because we have covered a long path. (Silence) What's the next plan?
Columbus	:	I think of the King of Portugal. What a betrayal! His councilors mocked me when I tried to explain my plan with

	a map at the Court of Portugal. But John understood the importance of my project. Without informing me, he sent a navigator for the discovery of India. But how can God tolerate this injustice?
Pynchon	: What happened next?
Columbus	: There was a massive whirlpool in the ocean. So he returned terrified. After that, John wrote a letter to me requesting for the sea voyage. After such a betrayal, how could I accept his request?
Pynchon	: Denying him, you have done an excellent job. He is responsible for this. All the faults lie in him. But instead, he is taking revenge on you.
Columbus	: I now wonder, instead of being ashamed of his actions to me, he becomes annoyed and revengeful.
Pinchon	: (Roaring of the storm) Admiral, the storm intensifies occasionally. It's raining non-stop. Again, it seems to start heavily from the north.
Columbus	: Yes, it's true. There will be heavy rainstorms. Everywhere, darkness prevails. For how many hours will it be continued?
Pynchon	: I am afraid of seeing these sea waves. You can watch how they are approaching us like a mountain. The ship trembles and gets imbalanced now. Anything can happen at any time-
Columbus	: Don't feel sick with apprehension. Our Jesus will save us. Had he not blessed us, I would not have joined this expedition despite

	my sorrow, poverty, disappointment and humiliation. You return to your ship now and order others to be alert and attentive. Again, make an arrangement to pray the ocean thrice a day.
Pynchon	: Then I leave now-
Columbus	: Yes, listen to me. There should be good preparation of food and drink from now onward. If they engross themselves in sumptuous meals and prayers, the navigators won't get time to think of the dangerous situations. (Sea roaring)
Announcement	: Please pass the information to the navigators of Ninja, Pinta and Santa Maria ships that they will be vigilant regarding the storm situation. There should not be any apprehension. There is nothing to be afraid of right now. So, to remove fear from crew members' minds, they have to do the sea prayer thrice a day.

(The prayer is sung in chorus loudly.)
O Lord! This blue ocean is your manifestation!
Your compassion lies here with the waves in unison.
Like the light in darkness assures faith and conviction;
and shows this man to move on right path and direction.
Because of you, we can overcome storms and danger,
And pilot the ship to stand safe on the sea beach ever.

SCENE-VI

Navigator I : Columbus says, 'within a few days, the tornado will disappear.' But why doesn't it subside?

Navigator II : Do you think that the tornado will vanish quickly? He has diverted our mind from the main course of action.

Navigator I : Then what shall we do? O Lord-

Navigator II : At last, we will die in the palace of the sea monsters. You can see from the very beginning how we see the ill omens. Were our parents and grandparents stupid? Why had they not displayed their bravery to cross the Atlantic Ocean? Don't you know that the sea monsters will raise storm first in the sea? Those who return, are aware of their presence, and will save everything. But they won't leave the obstinate people like us and throw us into the unfathomable depths of the ocean.

Navigator I : The intensity of the rainstorm increases every hour. It does not subside at all. The monsters are showing their annoyance.

Navigator II	: Won't they be angry? How will they tolerate while we, the people, are travelling over their heads?
Navigator I	: If there's a sky-touching wave at any moment, we will be nowhere-
Navigator II	: Knowingly, we show our neck to *Yamraj* (We are inviting death.) He will harness our movement. When he pulls the rein fastened to our neck, we have to follow him.
Navigator I	: Right you are! *Yamraj*, in the guise of Columbus, is directing us towards the hell.
Navigator II	: We have patience to some extent. But the condition of many people on the ship is horrible. Everyone hears the same story: "Some of them are invoking Lord Jesus earnestly; some are pouring tears thinking of their families, some are losing their sense, and some are talking loquaciously."
Navigator I	: Is there any way out? Columbus is not listening to us at all. He is constantly reminding us of the King's Punishment.
Navigator II	: Because of the King's decree, we have come. Otherwise-

SCENE-VII

Columbus : Brothers! I can understand your state of mind. You are all terrified by this severe cyclonic storm. But, mind it; I am hardly affected by its intensity. The cause for this is that I have strong faith in the most compassionate God, Lord Jesus. Had we not been blessed by Him, our ships would not have moved very fast towards the point of destiny like the arrows despite the Natural Calamity. We have not been born here on this earth to be satisfied with the least. We have come to the world to gather more wealth, success and fame. But for this, we have to undergo a stern test. This situation today we are experiencing is of that kind. God takes this test to study our strength of mind. We have to get through the ordeal. We must prove to the world that we are not timid and cowardly. We must break through the shackles of superstitions that have existed in the world for ages.

Navigator I	: If we lose our life! Man works hard for this life.
Navigator II	: We pray to God day and night. But there is improvement of the situation. Who knows whether there is a blessing or curse for us?
Columbus	: Have patience. You will surely understand the importance of my words one day.
Navigator I	: Admiral, you don't tell us about patience. We have already spent several days having faith in you. Don't lead us to the hell of death, please. We humbly request you folding our palms. Please give us the order to send back our ships.
Navigator II	: Do you realize there's no terrestrial land before us?
Columbus	: There is a terrestrial land. Is the information prescribed in the Geography Book wrong? You can understand this very well from this map whether any terrestrial land is or not after this great ocean. Can we think of any creation without the terrestrial land? I request you all to have your patience. Face the reality with courage. God has created Man to be the winner, not to accept defeat and surrender helplessly. One who accepts defeat has no place to live in this world. The creation is only for the winners.
Navigator I	: We need the mind to understand this philosophy. What we see before us–
Columbus	: Hear me, I am telling my story. Am I not afraid of my life? Then, why am I not

withdrawing myself? I firmly believe, "After a thousand of failures, the success will come." There is no need to be worried. I have already tasted this in my life. Earlier to my visit to Spain, my proposal for a sea voyage was placed before the courts of Portugal, Genoa, and Venice. For this, I have established good relationships with many people, run frequently, succumbed to pressure from many angles, and you can't imagine how much I have spent. But what have I received instead? I have returned from everywhere with disappointment, humiliation, and criticism. Forgetting the past and selling what I was with, I have sent my brother Bartholomew to the Court of England with my proposal. The pirates of the sea trapped him. I didn't get any information about him for one month. Then, I bravely got through the stages of experiencing the heavy interest of loans, cruel poverty, loss of my life, and the responsibility of maintaining my motherless child. Can you think of the mental state that I was undergoing in that situation? Anybody other than me could have done the suicide. I had not been disheartened. I continued my efforts consistently. As earlier, with solid perseverance, waiting for the rainy days to end, I finally reached the Court of Spain. On my first attempt, I was insulted there and returned. But there was the

	blessing of God, and I became successful in the end.
Navigator II	: Why are you comparing you with us? You and us-
Columbus	: Why do you think that you and I are different? I was also a typical navigator like you one day. If I am elevated to a higher position, it's because of my moral courage.
Navigator I	: Our mind gets weakened, though we try very hard.
Columbus	: Do your duties believing me. We will reach the 'Land of Gold' India shortly. There, you will see the pieces of gold are scattered everywhere. One who wants any amount can bring home. After we return, we will be the wealthiest people in our country. Can you think of wealth and prestige simultaneously in future?
Navigator II	: If we get huge pieces of gold, our social prestige will also reach the peak. The people will look at us and get surprised if we walk on the road.
Navigator I	: Forget about the outsiders? At our home, we will be worshipped like deities. What will I do on the very first day? I will sleep raising a small embankment of gold around the bed.
Navigator II	: You all join the work. Some more days are to pass. If you work hard for a few days, you don't have to work hard for your entire life.
Navigator I	: We will certainly reach the 'Land of Gold' one day.

SCENE-VIII

Columbus : So many weeks passed. How will I pacify the navigators, alluring them with false promises? They have started disbelieving me gradually. One day, they will know that I am doing wrong calculations in the Log Book regarding the coverage of distance. At any moment, they may revolt against me. There is no end to sabotage work. The navigators directing the ship curb the prows of ships northeastward every day. Had they not been red-handed, the situation could have been disastrous. (Silence) O Lord! What's in my fate? Is it true that my life lamp will be extinguished in this vast ocean? Why did you bring me to such a distance if that was your wish? I have spent so many sleepless nights. But where's the sea coast? It's relatively easy to struggle against Nature. But, it's very difficult and dangerous to fight against some uninterested co-travelers.

SCENE-IX

Navigator I	: O brother! You see how two birds are flying over our ships. How strange their bodies are!
Navigator II	: What do you say? Birds? Where? Where are they?
Navigator I	: See here. Where are you watching? Look at this side only.
Navigator II	: Yes, it's true. We are nearing the coast. Otherwise, where would we see the birds? How will the flying birds stay in this great ocean?
Navigator I	: O Lord! Are we approaching the 'Land of Gold'?
Navigator II	: That day, having seen the broken mast, we were all terrified. We all thought, "Who can say that our ships won't attend this stage one day?"
Navigator I	: We are not afraid of, Brother! We have suffered a lot. Bad time goes, good time comes in. Please, you see how the storm has subsided simultaneously.
Navigator II	: O, look at the sky on the left side. There is a giant comet. It's extended up to the sea.

Navigator I	: Brother, everything is over. Why were we happy few minutes earlier? We can't escape the comet. It symbolizes evil signs. We are still determining the events happening next.
Navigator II	: As we have seen the comet, the hopes of our life get diminished.
Navigator I	: If we love to live, let's return from this place. We can't.
Navigator II	: At dawn yesterday, I had a bad dream. I am not well for the whole day. In the dream, I saw my little daughter crawling toward the well. Her mother is absent-minded. From a distance, having seen her, I ran. No sooner did I reach there than she had dropped. I am shouting. Can you say why I had a horrible dream like this? After crawling, my daughter was standing intermittently. Now, she must be walking.
Navigator I	: The dream may not be true. We are experiencing a very tough time. I am unable to sleep, how can I see dreams? As if I was turning into a machine. I have forgotten everything: Trees, soil, wheat fields, and grape creepers- (At this time, everybody is shouting. Who speaks what needs to be clarified.) Comet? A comet is visible in the sky. Please see the comet. It generally indicates an ill omen. Our death time is indeed nearing. If we move ahead, there

	is no escape. Pass the information to the Admiral. Let's stop our work. The ships should not move at all. We will return the vessel forcibly. We may suffer for our whole life in jail as Punishment. We don't have fear now. Today, we have yet to be ready to obey anybody.
Columbus	: Oh! Why are you shouting? Nothing wrong is happening, having seen the comet. What's strange about it?
Navigator I	: Please, order us to return our ships, Admiral. We are not ready to march ahead.
Columbus	: I don't know why superstitions and blind beliefs regulate your mind. How do you think of returning after covering a long distance? Can you bear the shame and insult we will receive if we return now? It's a hundred times better to face death than to tolerate crooked mockeries of the people. Who knows what Punishment we will get after returning from this spot? Being annoyed, the King may give us life imprisonment or Capital Punishment. (Then, from the top of the mast is heard- "The terrestrial land is visible now. The land is visible from such a long distance.")
Navigator I	: This is the terrestrial land!
Columbus	: Terrestrial Land. O savior Lord! You save us now!
Navigator II	: Speed up the ships forward. The coast lies ahead. (There is clamour, a cry of happiness and a ringing of the bell for prayer.)

SCENE-X

Columbus : What a misfortune! A large cloud is the terrestrial land from a distance. That cloud disappears gradually in the broad day light. What's the mystery of God? How many days? For how many days will I threaten them and mislead their minds? (The vessel puffs her sail again.)

Columbus : Our ships now enter the extensive grassland. At that time, having seen the blunted plateau, you were surprised. Now you see.

Navigator I : Is this the terrestrial land, Sir?

Columbus : It's not. But the sea is shallow here. That's why the grassland is observed. The terrestrial land is not far away.

Navigator I : The grassland is so dense that it's very tough to pilot the ship.

Columbus : Here, you all have to put in some extra effort. What shall we do?

Navigator II : Sir, is this the country of snakes?

Columbus : Who says? Where will the snakes come from?

Navigator II : The older men are telling, by Nature, that

	the snakes are nocturnal. In day time, they won't come out. At night, they will come thousands from the grassland. Can you think of what will be our condition at that time?
Navigator I	: You are also under delusion by the words of older men. When the older men are present-
Columbus	: No need to fear. Our ships will stay here. Throwing the anchor into the grassland, we will take a rest here.
Navigator I	: Then we are getting down. We will take a bath for a while. We have not poured a drop of water on our bodies. We will enjoy it. If we don't swim-
Columbus	: Get down, those who wish to—no more water at the grassland. The weather is also excellent and temperate.

SCENE-XI

Navigator II	: Admiral, Admiral! Try to make the arrangements of leaving the place. Here is a great danger.
Columbus	: What has happened?
Navigator	: Sea witches?
Columbus	: Sea witches?
Navigator II	: Yes, Sir. Now, my body trembles in fear.
Columbus	: Tell me what happened there.
Navigator II	: While dipping in the sea we bathed, I felt something like a patch of grass in my hands. While pulling that, someone got hold of my legs. Experiencing that patch, I came out of the water and saved my life. Otherwise, the sea witch-
Columbus	: All right! Ha…ha…ha… (Laugh)
Navigator II	: Don't laugh, Sir. Under the sea surface, a thousand of sea witches are sleeping. They have been informed that we have reached here. If they get up, we will lose our lives.
Columbus	: I am confused now whether I will smile or cry, having heard you. Who has instilled

	this idea into your head? Well, you see how three beautiful birds have perched on the ship's mast.
Navigator II	: Yes, true.
Columbus	: Now you can realize that the terrestrial land is nearby. Birds are not the aquatic animals. They take rest on the trees of any land.
Navigator II	: Yes, you are right. Wherefrom have they come? Is this not a magic of the witches?
Columbus	: Again, the same story of witches and the magic. I see, it's very tough to control you.
Navigator II	: Sir, you see now. You didn't believe magic. No clouds were seen in the sky a few minutes earlier. Everywhere the sun shined brightly. At once, a big black cloud floated in the sky. Where did it come from?
Columbus	: Again, there will be a rainstorm. What a surprise! The nice weather has changed suddenly. (All the people on the ship start shouting.-"Here is a storm again. Oh, what a rainfall! There is no escape. Oh, we have already reached the 'Land of Gold' to garner the gold pieces. Your greed for gold has brought you to this land. Now you all die. It's right to all of you.")
Columbus	: Oh-why do you all lose your patience? We must control the situation.
Navigator II	: How can we control? We are already on the horns of a dilemma and wondering what to do next. (The rainstorm roars in the sky.)

Columbus : Again, calamity! Is there no end to natural disasters? While we see a ray of light in deep darkness, that light has sunk into some nether world, too.

SCENE-XII

Teacher: There is a strong conspiracy against Columbus. He overcomes every moment the chaotic confused state of expectation, apprehension, hope, and fear. It's the very critical moment of his life. The brutal mockery of Nature has shattered all his dreams. Now, all the navigators believe that the coast is impossible if we move along. After some days, we will have no food. We are going to die without food in the sea. So, the only way to solve the problem is to murder the stubborn guy Columbus. They have decided- in the dreary darkness, while Columbus observes the distant sky standing near the railing, he will be abruptly pushed into the sea. Fortunately, they have yet to come forward to do so. But they all plan to assault Columbus collectively. By God's grace, at the right moment, Columbus becomes aware of all the navigators' mental states and their evil plans.

SCENE-XIII

[The last part of the prayer comes to an end indistinctly. At this time, it is heard in the audience-"No, we won't hear anything...no, we won't hear anything...no, we won't hear anything..."]

Navigator I : We have come here unitedly to know your last decision whether you will return the ships or not.

Columbus : No, The vessels can't return unless these reach the coast. Impossible!

Navigator I : We haven't come here to be silent because of your browbeating and intimidation. We have come here to find the last solution to this critical situation. We will decide at this moment.

Columbus : What kind of solution do you need?

Navigator I : Solution? It's what you have never expected to hear from us. We can clarify, "If you consider our life very insignificant, we won't retreat to consider your life so."

Columbus : Is this your last decision?

Navigator I : Yes.

Columbus : I would also like to thank you for this adventurous step. It's elementary to murder me. I am also ready to embrace death every moment. But have you ever thought of its consequences? You have not considered the punishment you will face if you kill a representative of the Royal Court. Remember that I have not come here for my work. At the cost of my life, I have decided firmly to enhance the pride of Spain. Are Spain's wealth, beauty, honour and dignity not yours? You may have different opinions, but the King is the country's ruler where you are all the subjects. You have come here with me to fulfill this objective. You can decide if you deviate from this by any betrayal or conspiracy, the consequence you will have later. You are the decision makers for this. I am not. (Silent) One more point:
Have you calculated how far we have covered the sea and the paths? Can you return to your country without my help? I don't have any say if you choose to move on the dangerous path instead of the better one. Remember, so many lives don't get lost in the great ocean aimlessly. (Silent) Having perceived your evil plans, I have sympathy for you. What do you think that I am insolent to understand your mind and sentiments? I know what circumstances have brought you all to such a long distance. Brothers,

I am not cruel and brutal. I am also equally unhappy like you. I also love my life. I have also love and affection for my friends and relatives. I am not mad. Please, believe me and leave to me your sorrows and happiness. I stand before you all very calmly with my presence of mind. At a small distance a vast land waits anxiously to welcome us. Like the sea, like the sky, that land mass is also true. Can't we patiently wait some days more to experience this Truth wholeheartedly? (Pynchon's voice is heard from a distance.)

Pynchon : Land Mass. Land Mass. Please see here. The land mass is visible.

Columbus : The land mass is visible. Is it true?

Navigator I : Can you say where the land mass is? (A clamour)

Navigator II : Is it true that the ships touch the coast? Where? Nothing is visible?

Navigator I : O Lord, You are most compassionate!

Columbus : Well, I am going to the top of the mast. It will be seen clearly through a telescope. Lord, our life's protector, will help us reach the goal. All of you can start the sea prayer. I will return shortly.
(They all start singing the prayer unitedly.)

Navigator I : Is the coast visible, Admiral?

Columbus : No, I can't see anything. That may be the coast. Once the night ends, I can confirm you. Everything will be apparent in sunlight.

Navigator II	: Is it not the mirage as earlier stated?
Columbus	: No, this time near the horizon, the coastline is marked. Now I can't confirm you. Then you know this much that the coastline is close to us.
Navigator II	: Let's see what's in our luck.
Columbus	: Yes, I still need to tell you one more point. Before we started our expedition, the Great Empress Isabella told me to announce before all the navigators of three ships. Out of you, who will reach the terrestrial land first will be rewarded ten thousand gold coins. He will be honoured with this reward every year at the court. Be alert for this. Let's see who will be that lucky guy. (Silence) yes, this was the reward of the Empress. I have also planned to give him a gift personally. It will be an ordinary gift, but a costly red coat. (A clamour of happiness)
Navigator I	: Speed up the ships.
Navigator II	: Come, please come. You all have to join together.

SCENE-XIV

Columbus : I have come to call you Captain Pynchon.
Pynchon : Please tell me. How can I help you?
Columbus : When you told your navigators that the coast is visible, they were thrilled and excited that day. But, we are unfortunate. What we thought of as the terrestrial land was a cloud. I am still consoling the navigators that we are very close to the sea coast.
Pynchon : I have also told the same to all my navigators. For how many days will we mislead and befool them? They are also getting disappointed day by day. If, in a few days-
Columbus : I can understand their state of mind, Pynchon. What shall I do? All these are out of my control. Their breathings have stabbed me time and again when they breathe long, staying at a distance. But what's the other alternative? We are helpless. Now, I don't have any way out except having faith in God.
Pynchon : The navigators become rude day by day.

	There is no decency in their behaviour. I am listening to what they speak. But I don't dare to tell them hard.
Columbus	: Even in my Santa Maria ship, a similar situation pervades. Who can say what the people will do at any moment, how they have been disappointed and lost their patience? The aggrieved people become satanic in their approach. I don't have any hope, even from the most trusted ones. They have started suspecting me— an inner stream of revolt hikes against me among the navigators. At any moment, I may face a group assault.
Pynchon	: The situation is going to be critical day by day-
Columbus	: You have to do one work. You try to reinforce and boost the navigators of my ship with moral courage. They may alleviate themselves after hearing you.
Pynchon	: I will try my best with the bit of energy I have, if anything happens. I am also harassed.
Columbus	: You can't understand my state of mind. Sometimes, I feel that I am getting mad. Had I been a lunatic in true sense, it would have been better.
Pynchon	: If your state of mind becomes so-
Columbus	: No, it's temporary. But I am all right, fantastic. Despite all this, with patience, I sincerely execute my duties. I have never allowed others to study my mind.
Pynchon	: Who will speak?

Columbus	: But it's my firm conviction that we must overcome the waves of time like the sea waves. (The navigators march ahead with their slogan.) The ambassador of death, Columbus-stay away, The exploiter, Columbus- We won't obey your command or follow your order. We'll send back our ships forcibly; we'll send back our vessels.
Pynchon	: (Shouting) Brothers, be calm! Be quiet!
Navigator II	: We have yet to come here to be quiet. Today, we are here to send back the ships forcibly.
Columbus	: It's not the right time to send back the ships.
Navigator II	: We won't hear anything. We will neutralize the person who will obstruct us.
Columbus	: This is the same old question. We can't solve the question out of unnecessary excitement.
Navigator I	: How many days will you continue your pretence?
Columbus	: Anyway we are still striving for a solution.
Navigator I	: On behalf of the navigators, there is one question for you: whether you will choose life or death. Out of these two, what will you select?
Pynchon	: What do you say now? Please listen to me.

Salabega and Columbus | 117

Navigator II	: Who has told you to be the broker of Columbus? Please return to your ship, or else you join us. Otherwise, you will face what Columbus is experiencing.
Columbus	: At my death, will all your problems be solved? Are you all of this opinion?
Navigator I	: Yes, today, we all have one common opinion and one voice.
Columbus	: I tell you frequently, "I have already made a promise in life to play with death." At this moment, I am dead, and it won't move me. But man's ignorance and surrender before Nature will appeal to me. On the other side of the ocean lies a massive terrestrial land that will be unexplored forever. That's why I pray to you all with folding palms. Let me give you five more days. I will submissively accept your punishment if I don't show you the new land within four days.
Pynchon	: Please don't make this kind of promise, Admiral! A man should not be so confident about Nature.
Columbus	: Truth is tough to bear, Captain. For the establishment of Truth, the blind earth wants the sacrifice or life of some people like me. It's not surprising at all.
Pynchon	: You are generous, you are great.
Columbus	: Brothers! Are you prepared to give four days to me? (All are silent.) Why are you silent? I will never force you to share your independent opinions.
Navigator I	: So many days have already passed. What

            will be our loss if we wait for four days more?
Columbus   : Well, I am happy to know your state of mind.

SCENE-XV

Columbus : This is the fourth day of my promise. It's 11 October 1492. In darkness, three ships are marching ahead like the meteors. I am pleased. The blue sky is over our heads, and the blue-white sea lies before us. Showering blessing, the bright silvery moon rises in the East. The twinkling stars reflect on the sea. The birds in groups return to their nests with lots of hopes and consolation. What a strange, beautiful scene! Having seen this picturesque view, I want to know why I am overwhelmed with sublime peace and heavenly bliss. Now, I can realize the blessings of Lord Jesus by his hand-waving.

(There is heard the splashing of the ships.)

Columbus : You can now see a big tree branch beside Ninja ship.

Navigator I : Show me that. Where?

Columbus : Let the navigators of the Ninja ship be informed to pick up that branch floating near the ship.

Navigator I	: (Shouting) Roderigo, a raw branch of a tree is floating beside your ship. Please pick it up. Pick up. It's the fresh branch of a tree. It's full of berries.
Columbus	: Right now, do you believe that the terrestrial land is very close to us? Where will we get trees unless there is the land? Well, call everybody to come here. Come here to see. Who is there? Look at this direction. There seems to be a light. Can you see how it's flickering?
Navigator I	: Yes, Sir. There is a bonfire. Where does the fire come from? The people must have set the fire.
Navigator II	: Is it fire?
Navigator I	: What's this? The fire is not visible now. Is it extinguished?
Navigator II	: Where is the fire? It's false. The light you have seen may be of the witches. Had it not been of witches, how could it have been extinguished? We are now entering the Kingdom of Ghosts. We will die while watching their magic. It's the Truth. (At this time, the firing of Pinta's ship is heard. Then suddenly, the people of that ship start shouting.)
All	: Now we have reached the coast. All should get up. We have reached the shore.
Navigator I	: The people of Pinta ship see the coastline first. (Then there is a great round of applause at once, singing and dancing with rhythms. The sea prayer echoes.)

SCENE-XVI

Columbus : It's the early morning of 12 October 1492. Today, we have reached the vast terrestrial land. Looking at the surroundings, we perceive and enjoy the panoramic beauty of Nature here. The most pleasant greenery of Earth Queen is always eye-catching and appealing. I don't have the power to express my indescribable happiness in language. It's the spiritual bliss. I am gradually forgetting myself. Because of God's infinite power, I am completely overwhelmed. Our long journey is successful today. Moving away from the darkness of happiness, Man has extended his right or authority over Nature. Because of that blessing, the flag of Spain is hoisted above freely. Come closer to me, you all. (Silent) My Brothers! You have all come, leaving behind your wife, sons, parents, and relatives, forgetting the subtle illusion and fighting with the sea day and night. I wholeheartedly accept your sorrows,

	sufferings, and the perseverance of your efforts. It's not my victory but yours. I am ever grateful to you. In this auspicious moment I embrace you all from the inner core of my heart. I will be happy in my heart and soul. (Silent) Brothers! Columbus bows down before you for the cruelty and inhumanity displayed earlier. Columbus is not heartless and inconsiderate. You see today how his heart is full of love and excitement.
Teacher	: Has the spell of the play ended? Nothing is surprising. The Columbuses take birth on this indifferent earth at every age. They want to explore life in danger and misery and are not interested in enjoying an easy and peaceful life. Before them, victory and defeat and profit and loss are all equal. For them, the other name of life is adventurous battle and expedition.

****

APPENDIX

Hymn:
āhe nīḷa saiḷa prabaḷa matta bārana
By Salabega

āhe nīḷa saiḷa prabaḷa matta bārana
mo arata naḷinī banaku kara daḷana / Refrain/

gajarāja chintā kalā thāi ghora jaḷeṇa
chakra pesi nakra nāsi uddhārila āpaṇa /1/

ghora bane mruguṇi-ki paḍithila kasaṇa
keḍe baḍa bipatti-ru rakhyā kala āpaṇa /2/

kuru-sabhā tale suni dropadi-ra jaṇāṇa
koti bastra dei hele lajjā kala bāraṇa /3/

rābaṇa-ra bhāi bibhīsana gala saraṇa
saraṇa sambhāḷi tānku lanke kala rājana /4/

prahallāda pitā se je baḍa dusta dāruṇa
stambha-ru bāhāri tāku bidārila takhyaṇa /5/

kahe sālabega hina jāti-re mun jabana
sriraṅgā charaṇa tale karu-achi jaṇāṇa /6/

Black Eagle Books

www.blackeaglebooks.org
info@blackeaglebooks.org

Black Eagle Books, an independent publisher, was founded as a nonprofit organization in April, 2019. It is our mission to connect and engage the Indian diaspora and the world at large with the best of works of world literature published on a collaborative platform, with special emphasis on foregrounding Contemporary Classics and New Writing.

www.ingramcontent.com/pod-product-compliance
Lightning Source LLC
Chambersburg PA
CBHW060616080526
44585CB00013B/849